'Se
Fir

St. Giles' Parish Church, Matlock

'Seek Ye First . . .'
The Gospel and Moral Choices

Editors: John Greenhalgh and Elizabeth Russell

St Mary's, Bourne Street

To
Father John Gilling
with grateful thanks for
twenty years' ministry at
St Mary's, Bourne Street

First published 1992
St Mary's, Bourne Street
St Mary's Presbytery
30 Bourne Street
London SW1W 8JJ

ISBN 0 9508516 5 5

British Library Cataloguing-in-Publication Data
A catalogue record for this book is available from the British Library

Phototypeset in Souvenir and Times by Intype, London
Printed in Great Britain by Page Bros, Norwich

Foreword

by the Bishop of London

OVER THE YEARS St Mary's, Bourne Street has sponsored the publication of material which has always contributed very significantly to Christian reflection, understanding and exploration.

These present articles are no less important. They address a range of moral issues with a depth of insight and theological perception. As well there is a refreshing realism about the difference and diversity of views and approaches currently abroad in the Church and in society.

Here are contributions from a variety of writers which reflect a serious approach to the moral issues they raise. They will surely help every Christian person who, given the demands of the gospel and the realities of human weakness and sinfulness, nevertheless seeks ever to be faithful to the new and living way which is offered through baptism into the death and resurrection of Jesus.

✠ *David Londin:*

PURE IN POWER

Will
women,
men,
who can
hold in the hollow of the heart
the lapis lazuli of night
win?
when
hurt
not
harm
any
one?

JONATHAN GRIFFIN
10·XI·80

6

Contents

Part III: Some moral dilemmas

Preface

Bill Scott

OUR SERIES of St Mary's **Tracts for Our Times** began with the celebration of the 150th anniversary of the Oxford Movement and the recalling of the famous tracts which had great influence on the thoughts and beliefs of many in the Church of England and beyond. This is now the sixth in the series, which has addressed contemporary issues concerning the Church in our time. Since John Greenhalgh and Elizabeth Russell took over the editorship the Tracts have explored faith, praxis and mission. In *'If Christ be not risen . . .'* there was a stimulating discussion on the resurrection faith central to our Christian belief. The customs and practice of the sacramental life were examined in *Signs of Faith, Hope and Love. Building in Love* sought to respond to the decade of evangelisation. Our attention is now turned to the morality and ethics of our day.

This subject is not unrelated to these other topics and is one which troubles and concerns many people, not least ordinary parish priests like myself, who struggle not only with the difficulties of living a Christian life style personally in a secularised society, but who often have to teach and advise others about the 'Christian' way. There can be a great divide between the pastoral and the ethical. This is highlighted in the story told by the novelist, Bruce Marshall, in *All Glorious Within* contrasting responses of an Anglican dignitary and a Roman Catholic dignitary on passing a prostitute in the street. The former raises his hat and says, 'Not tonight, dear'; the latter says, 'You'll roast like a faggot'. As my own approach has always been remarkably Anglican in this respect, it is good to have a series of articles which stretch the mind and encourage us to think about and face issues of morality.

The symposium begins with thinking about God. The theological statements cover a wide range of topics from the general philosophy of morality to the theology of creation. In the second part we find people with very specialist interests and skills examining living issues.

Part three presents us with real grounded dilemmas, almost case studies, of a non-theoretical nature. The subject of legislating for a Christian morality in a diverse society is examined in the interview with David Alton. We are very grateful to all the contributors who have given freely of their services to this publication. Their generosity along with the hard work of the editors has made this publication possible. The distinguished poet, the late Jonathan Griffin, was a member of St Mary's congregation and wrote the previously unpublished poem, *Pure in Power*, our frontispiece, after a visit to the shrine of our Lady at Walsingham. We are pleased to have a foreword by the Bishop of London who has shown a great interest in our parish.

The life style of the follower of Christ is a response to the gospel of love. Since the Second Vatican Council the approach of moral theologians seems to have become much more inspired by the spirit of the gospel; by the approach of Jesus who in the Sermon on the Mount gives us no legalistic moral code, but a vision of life in the kingdom of God. Although not attainable by most mortal creatures, his teaching is there to inspire and encourage us towards being people whose love, like his own, knows no bounds. The heart of our 'spiritual' journey is an opening up of our very beings to receive the love of God in all its fullness. It is only as we are transformed by love that our actions can truly be described as right and that very transformation will have an effect more than we will realise on the life and morality of others. Remember, also, if this seems too difficult, that it is not empty rhetoric which causes Jesus to say that prostitutes and tax-gathers will attain to the kingdom first. Our very sinfulness and weakness can be a means of growing in God's love because we know the shallowness of our own.

My prayer is that those who read this book will be inspired to think and ponder over the deep matters of personal and corporate behaviour and attitudes and will discover something of that great love flowing from the Godhead which, when they receive it, will help them to help others to live life in all its fullness.

Bill Scott is parish priest of St Mary's, Bourne Street.

The moral teaching of Jesus in the contemporary world

John Macquarrie

Morality and human nature

MANY PEOPLE think that we are living in a time of moral decline. It is indeed the case that many moral conventions which were generally accepted even a generation ago are now being set aside, and those who still observe them are frequently dismissed as 'old-fashioned' in their views. To give a fairly obvious example, many of us alive today remember when abortion was considered to be a particularly odious crime. Today, thousands of abortions are carried out in our hospitals as an accepted routine. Back in the 1930s, a very few people were prepared to argue that in certain circumstances, for instance, after a rape, the termination of a pregnancy might be an acceptable procedure. But now the circumstances need not be exceptional at all. We have been living since the 1960s in a 'permissive' society, and such a society inevitably leads to a decline of moral standards. If people are told that such-and-such behaviour is permissible, many will think it is actually being encouraged, or, at the very least, there is no harm in it. Many other factors have contributed in recent decades to the downgrading of morality, such as the weakening of religious authority, the reluctance to give any clear moral or religious teaching in schools, the disruption of families and so on.

But I do not think that this process of moral decline will go on indefinitely. Already people are getting worried about the soaring crime rates in the secularised cities of the western world. A point will come when a reaction will take place. The reason for saying this, and saying it with confidence, is that the human being is by nature a being for whom moral issues are inescapable. Even if many of the things we do are a result of our genetic inheritance and others a result of social pressures, there is an area where we have to make our own responsible choices, an area where we have to choose between right and wrong, good and bad. Each one of us has a conscience, and sometimes we go against it. But it is perhaps rare for anyone simply to flout his or her conscience. It forces us to consider what we are doing, to think about the effects of what we are doing on ourselves or on other people.

For many centuries, moral philosophers have talked about 'natural law'. By that expression, they have meant that in our own human nature there is a kind of law, that directs us, if we will attend to it, toward a more human, more fulfilling life, both for ourselves and for society. Where does this natural law come from? Perhaps first of all from thousands of years of human experience, in which people have learned what leads to a fuller, more satisfying humanity, and what leads on the other hand to diminished forms of human life. Perhaps more ultimately this natural law comes from God. In biblical teaching, human beings were made in the image of God, and it is this image deep within us that we experience as conscience directing us to some kinds of behaviour rather than others. Now, although moral conventions have differed at different times in history and still do differ among diffe rent nations and different cultures, there are great areas of agreement among all peoples – Christians, adherents of non-Christian religions, and serious people who may not profess any religion. Although they may not in fact obey it, they all have a moral sense, an awareness of the obligation to seek the good and avoid the evil.

This inbuilt sense of obligation that we call natural law is the foundation of all morality and is assumed in all particular moral codes. In different cultures it finds different expressions but unless there were this universal moral capacity in human beings, then no moral teaching could be appreciated and no particular system of morals could develop. This applies even to the moral teaching of Jesus. It does not exist in a vacuum. It was taught by one who had himself grown up in the lofty moral atmosphere of Judaism and in fact there are many parallels between the teaching which Jesus gave and that of other Jewish teachers. For example, when Jesus is asked what is the great commandment, he answers simply by quoting two verses from the Old Testament: 'You shall love the Lord your God with all your heart, and with all your soul, and with all your mind, and with all your strength.' And to this he added: 'You shall love your neighbour as yourself.' The first of these sentences is a quotation from the book of Deuteronomy, the second sentence is from Leviticus. Yet they are often treated as Jesus's own summary of his ethical teaching. The so-called Golden Rule, 'Whatever you wish that men would do to you, do so to them' (Matthew 7, 12), has been given prominence as an important saying of Jesus, but a very similar saying can be found in the Jewish book of Tobit, and other versions of the same idea occur in the sayings of world moral teachers from as far away as China. The moral teaching of Jesus therefore has the Jewish and Hebrew tradition as its background. With this comes, of course, the accompanying theology, belief in the one God and his governance of history.

The Jewish ethic presupposes the 'natural law' which runs through all the ethical systems of the human race. But superimposed on that natural law which goes back to the creation of humanity itself are many centuries or even millennia of development. During that long time, Jewish ethics took their distinctive shape. The most important moment in that long history was the giving of the law to Moses. Compressed into the Ten Commandments are some basic principles governing fundamental human behaviour. Just how fundamental these commandments are is shown by the fact that they survived into Christianity and are indeed known and respected as a kind of basic summary of morality through much of the civilized world. They reappear in the teaching of Jesus, although he felt himself free to revise or restate some of them quite drastically, as we shall see. The law of Moses was regarded by the Hebrew people as a revelation made specially to them by God. But the fact that the law of Moses was related to that fundamental moral law that is known to all peoples is clearly acknowledged by Paul, as a thoughtful Jew who was also acquainted with Greek thinking, in which natural law had an important place. So Paul writes: 'When Gentiles who have not the law do by nature what the law requires, they are a law to themselves, even though they do not have the law. They show that what the law requires is written on their hearts, while their conscience also bears witness and their conflicting thoughts accuse or perhaps excuse them' (Romans 2. 14–15).

It is true that the form which the law took in Israel, as summarised in the Ten Commandments, is mainly negative, for these commandments are primarily prohibitions. But, in the course of Israel's history, the code was gradually expanded to take in more moral questions. Eventually it is said to have included over six hundred commandments! Some of these were, of course, affirmative and the somewhat narrow and stern morality expressed in the Decalogue becomes much more humanistic when the Ten Commandments are seen in the wider context of Hebrew law as a whole. But even the use of the term 'law' can be misleading. It suggests a 'legalistic' mentality, overconcerned with details. No doubt this was true of some people, and we all know that Jesus criticised the Pharisees for their somewhat narrow legalism. But many Christians and other non-Jews have exaggerated the elements of legalism in the ethics of Israel and Judaism. Even in the Ten Commandments, moral and religious matters are mixed together, which means that the character of the God of the Old Testament, in whose image human beings are themselves supposed to be made, permeates the law as a whole. And that character is one in which grace and mercy have their place alongside justice. 'To the Lord our God belong mercy and forgiveness' (Daniel 9. 9). Recent biblical scholarship, especially the work of W. D. Davies and E. P. Sanders, has done much to dispel the idea, really a one-sided caricature, that Judaism promotes a harsh legalism and that Christianity, first in response to Jesus and then as taught by Paul, broke out of this into a religion of grace. The Hebrew word that is commonly translated into English as 'law', Torah, has the more fundamental meaning of 'instruction'. If you look up a Hebrew dictionary under this word, you will find that it was used for the instruction given by a parent to a child or by a prophet to the people or by a priest in his teaching about sacred things. In every synagogue the Torah is kept in a special receptacle and is treated with a reverence rather like that which Christians show towards the reserved sacrament in a church. The suggestion has even been made that one way of thinking of Jesus Christ would be to consider him an incarnation of the Torah, that is to say, a living manifestation of the Word of God, a conception which might to some extent bridge the gap between Christianity and Judaism.

If one were to attempt to summarise under a few broad headings the content of the Jewish ethic, perhaps the following points would convey its essence. At the heart of it is the **family**, both the duties of the parents to the children and of the children to their parents. This concern for the family is an obvious point of resemblance between Jews and Christians. Beyond the family lies the wider **community**, and, contrary to what is often believed, Jews are concerned not only with fellow-Jews but feel a responsibility also to strangers. This was a point where Jesus was deliberately concerned to open up the Jewish nation to the wider world, but the tendency was already there. The Jewish prophets laid great stress on securing justice for the **weaker members of society**, especially the poor and the handicapped. This is another point at which there is a clear continuity between the older teaching and the teaching of Jesus. Jews were very much concerned with the ethics of **property**, especially the care of the land and its preservation. This may have arisen from their doctrine of creation, for the land is finally God's land and deserves to be treated with respect. In this regard Jesus takes a somewhat different line for, although he was not an ascetic, he certainly did urge his followers not to be too anxious about material possessions.

If one wants to see the type of person who is produced by a faithful following of the Old Testament ethic, perhaps the best place to look is at the end of the book of Job. In Chapter 31 Job is making his defence before God, and he tells us what he has tried to do in his life and what he has tried to avoid. He has tried to discipline his sexual life, and to turn away from anything that might undermine good family relationships. He has avoided deceit and falsehood. He has listened to the complaints of his employees, for, he says, God has created both the master and the servant. He has tried to be generous to the poor, and has not tried to enjoy the blessings of food and shelter and other benefits without a thought for those who lack these things. Although he is a wealthy man, he has not made gold his trust as if it were more important than integrity. He has not rejoiced at the ruin of his enemies. He has been hospitable to strangers. He has not tried to conceal his faults but has been open about them. When it was right for him to speak out about something that was wrong or unjust, he has not kept silent, although it may have made him unpopular to say anything against what was going on. He is so confident of his righteousness that at the end he even becomes boastful. 'I would give God an account of all my steps,' he says, 'like a prince I would approach him.' Here we miss the humility which Jesus taught to his disciples.

But on the whole we are bound to acknowledge that this is an admirable and noble pattern of life that we see exemplified in Job, and our admiration increases when we realise that in spite of his moral rectitude, he suffered a great deal, but did not lapse into bitterness as so many would have done.

So all this accumulated moral wisdom, extending from the time of Moses right down to the Jews of Jesus' own time, is the background against which the moral teaching of Jesus was given. We can see that it is a very rich and full background, and that much of it deserved to be incorporated into any new teaching that Jesus would give. The Jews have always been specially interested in moral questions, and specially concerned to promote the moral life from generation to generation. Yet, one can say that this noble morality which they worked out in such detail is fundamentally the same as that 'natural law' which enters the constitution of every human being, just in virtue of the fact that he or she is a human being, made in the image of God. This is, if you like, the natural goal for every man and woman, the archetype of a truly human life. What then was there left for Jesus to do or to teach? I think perhaps we are given a clue in the title of a recent book by Anthony Harvey on the moral teaching of Jesus. He called it *Strenuous Commands*. It would need a strenuous effort to come anywhere near that natural ideal of the truly moral person that is taught by the Old Testament and that was realised in Job. Yet, however strenuous one's efforts, it seems to be always possible in human affairs to be just a little bit more strenuous. In the Olympic Games, each time a new record is set up, there eventually comes along a new competitor who cuts a bit off that record. Paul suggests that the Christian life is rather like taking part in a race and making a supreme effort to win. In the second part of this study of the moral teaching of Jesus, we shall see how he looked beyond even the high ideals of Judaism and called for something even more.

The new morality of Jesus

IN THE FIRST part of this essay, I tried to show that the morality taught by Jesus did not just suddenly appear from nowhere, but was brought forth within the context of the people of Israel with their long history of morality and spirituality, and that there was an even wider context, the context of 'natural law', that universal awareness of moral obligation that belongs to every nation and culture, indeed, one might say, to every normal individual man and woman. We saw that there are parallels between the teaching of Jesus and that of other great moral teachers of the past, but now I want to draw attention to what was new in Jesus' teaching, for this somewhat obscure figure from the obscure town of Nazareth was to become in course of time the best-known and most impressive teacher of morality in all human history. Also, we may say that no other teacher has so clearly lived out his teaching as Jesus did. The teaching that he gave was exemplified in his life, so that when one thinks of Jesus, one is less likely to think of what he said on this or that occasion than of the things that he did – healing the sick, serving his disciples, above all, dying on the cross for the sake of his mission. This is a teacher in whom there is no trace of the sin which he so severely condemned – that of hypocrisy. Life and teaching in him were one.

We have in fact already noted that one of the ways in which Jesus differed from the tradition in which he had grown up was to make the demands of morality more 'strenuous', to use the word which we found in Anthony Harvey. He was not the first to use this word about Jesus' teaching. Certainly Jesus' invitation to those whom he was calling to be his disciples indicated that they were being called to something very difficult. You might think that most people would be repelled rather than attracted by his words: 'If anyone would come after me, let him deny himself and take up his cross and follow me' (Mark 8. 34). For the disciple too, following Jesus was not just a matter of words, but a way of life. He or she was to take up the cross, not literally for most of them but certainly in a life of self-denial, as Jesus' own life had been.

The strenuousness of Jesus' teaching, the fact that he demands more than Moses and the teachers of old had demanded, is most clearly expressed in what are called the 'antitheses' (Matthew 5),

17

where Jesus quotes one of the ancient commandments and then proceeds to make it more strict. 'You have heard that it was said to the men of old, "You shall not kill" . . . but I say to you that everyone who is angry with his brother shall be liable to judgement.' Likewise, the men of old forbade adultery, but Jesus condemns the undisciplined desires that lie at the root of adultery and related offences. Again, the men of old prohibited perjury or swearing falsely, but Jesus says to his followers: 'Do not swear at all . . . Let what you say be simply "Yes" or "No" – anything more than this comes from evil.' Presumably he meant that it is only in a society where people profoundly distrust one another that oaths are needed; in any case, they do not succeed in safeguarding the truth, for only mutual trust can do that. As another example, he quotes the ancient principle: 'An eye for an eye and a tooth for a tooth.' This principle was originally intended to limit the retribution that might be demanded for an injury. That retribution could not go beyond the extent of the damage that had been suffered. But Jesus tells people to get away from the idea of retribution altogether. 'If someone strikes you on the right cheek, turn to him the other also. If someone takes your coat, give him your cloak as well.'

Who was this who publicly challenged the ancient laws and sought to revise them? Was he a radical, perhaps preaching an ideal anarchical society in which laws would no longer be needed? Matthew does not represent Jesus in that way. On the contrary, he reports Jesus as saying: 'Think not that I have come to abolish the law and the prophets. I have come not to abolish them but to fulfil them. For truly I say to you, till heaven and earth pass away, not an iota, not a dot, will pass from the law till all is accomplished. Whoever then relaxes one of the least of these commandments and teaches men so, shall be called least in the kingdom of heaven. For I tell you, unless your righteousness exceeds that of the scribes and Pharisees, you will never enter the kingdom of heaven.' In the early days of Christianity, there was much discussion about whether the law of Moses was still binding for Christians, or how much of it. It is difficult to know whether the words I have just quoted about the law truly represent what Jesus originally said, or whether they are Matthew's interpretation of what he believed Jesus to have said. Matthew had a good deal of sympathy for the Jewish tradition. Some scholars have claimed that he pictures Jesus as the new Moses. Just as Moses had given the law from Mount Sinai, so Jesus gives a new law which we know as the Sermon on the Mount. But the parallel between Jesus and Moses is not an exact one, and, in particular, the instruction which Jesus gives has a different form from the law of Moses, and could hardly be called a law. I think the most significant words in the introduction to the antitheses in Matthew's gospel is not what is said about the law's not being abolished but the final sentence that Jesus is said to have spoken to the disciples: 'For I tell you, unless your righteousness exceeds that of the scribes and Pharisees, you will never enter the kingdom of heaven.' That is to say, Jesus is making it clear that his demands are indeed strenuous and what he is asking will always be more than what would satisfy the demands of the traditional law.

For further clarification, we might consider an incident which is recorded in both Matthew's and Mark's gospels. I refer to the occasion when Jesus and his disciples were passing through the fields on a sabbath day, and plucked the ears of corn as they went along. Some Pharisees complained, and said to Jesus: 'Look, your disciples are doing what is not lawful to do on the sabbath.' Jesus defends the action of the disciples, and declares roundly: 'The sabbath was made for man, not man for the sabbath.' As we have seen, both religious and moral questions were embraced in the Jewish law, and Jesus' rejection of the sabbath law is usually interpreted as meaning that he did not wish to give permanence to religious observances peculiar to Judaism, as distinct from the moral teachings of the law of the Jews. But when Matthew tells this story, he leaves out the words about the sabbath being made for man, and this lends weight to the view that he did take a more sympathetic attitude to the law than most other New Testament writers.

But perhaps a more basic question has occurred to us as we think about these things. Does this revision of the law by Jesus, making it more difficult than it had hitherto been supposed to be, really make sense? We all know that usually, though it may sometimes require an effort, we can control our outward actions. Only a very few people commit murder or even serious physical assaults, and even they are more likely to do such things in a moment of passion than as a result of cold deliberation. If we switch our attention from murder and assault to adultery and sexual offences, more people are likely to commit these, but generally they are regarded as not quite so serious as violent offences aimed at the death or injury of another person. But when I ask whether Jesus' revision of the law making not only physical violence but anger, not only adultery but unrestrained desire, worthy of moral condemnation, is this not carrying the strenuous principle too far? For can we really control our passions? Do not anger and lust simply rise up unbidden in the human person, so how can they be blamed, especially if the person who has these feelings refuses to do the actions to which they are prompting him?

Perhaps the answer to this problem is to assert that even our passions can be brought under control, but this certainly needs time, and a process of training and formation. It is something in which we all need the help of other people, who are likely to be more aware of our weaknesses than we are ourselves. Hence the importance of education, in which children learn that it is good neither for themselves not for other people to have all their desires gratified. For adults it means that spiritual direction, which over the centuries has become part of the Christian spiritual tradition, should not be neglected.

The problem just noted is psychological rather than ethical. But one might claim that there are moral problems too with the strenuous demands of Jesus' teaching. Even if we could take them literally and obey them, would they not lead to the disruption of society? Let us suppose, for example, that when people were struck on the right cheek, it became a widespread response to adopt the Christian policy of turning the other cheek also, would this not simply encourage some members of society to attack others with impunity? And could there be any rights of property if a majority of people were prepared to give away their cloaks to those who robbed them of their coats? The simplest answer to this might be to say that the commands are being taken too literally. Jesus' words are being turned into new laws and interpreted in a legalistic fashion, whereas they were intended to be modifications of laws, pushing them in a more humanistic direction. There are other ways of looking at the problem.

At the beginning of this century, some New Testament scholars, including Albert Schweitzer, laid great stress on the fact that Jesus seemed to be expecting that the present world would come to an end very soon. The teaching of Jesus began from the claim: 'The time is fulfilled and the kingdom of God is at hand: repent, and believe the gospel' (Mark 1, 15). Schweitzer believed that Jesus' moral teaching has to be understood in the light of this expectation of a speedy end to the present world order – and this idea could be extended to other early Christian moral teaching including that of Paul. So Schweitzer said that the moral teaching of Jesus is, to use his expression, an *interim ethic*, a special kind of conduct not meant to be practised universally but applying to the short period remaining between the time when the teaching was given and the end of the present world which would also be the inauguration of the kingdom of God. When in fact the end of the world did not come as speedily as expected – and, indeed, has not yet come – there is a real problem about what the Church can do with this moral teaching of Jesus. The interim period is over and was not really an interim at all. So was the teaching given for the interim made obsolete when the end failed to happen? In that case, can we nowadays just forget about the Sermon on the Mount? That would be a strange conclusion, for it is precisely the Sermon on the Mount that has seemed to many people the highest reach of Christian teaching. However, the difficulties that arise out of Schweitzer's teaching have meant that very few people have followed him. Another great New Testament teacher of the twentieth century, Rudolf Bultmann, although he agreed with Schweitzer that Jesus' teaching was coloured throughout by an expectation of the end of the age, did not agree that this made it only an interim ethic with a temporary validity. On Bultmann's view, it should be understood as a call for 'radical obedience'. It is not so much a new or a special ethic as a radicalising, a deepening, of the moral demand that had come down in the Jewish tradition that had also, even if in less definite terms, come down in the traditions of all peoples because of their sharing in the natural law. When, however, one speaks of radical obedience, is one still speaking of a moral demand that is to be universalised? Even if it is addressed to all human beings and even if it were to be accepted by all in some ideal kingdom of God, could it be universally practised on this earth, or would that lead to social disruption, as we saw reason to suspect?

Here, I think, we have to study more closely what is meant by that expression which runs all through the teaching of Jesus – 'the kingdom of God'. There has, of course, been endless argument over the phrase. Some have thought of the kingdom as an ideal society to be realised on earth, and this idea has been revived in recent years in political theology and liberation theology. But there is very little support for such an interpretation in the New Testament itself, which seems to think of the kingdom as something that God himself will bring. Still, there is an ambiguity in sayings about the kingdom. Sometimes it seems to refer to a future reality beyond our earthly horizons, sometimes it is suggested that the kingdom is already among us, indeed, that Jesus himself has brought the kingdom. That ambiguity may well be deliberate. The kind of relations described in the Sermon on the Mount could hardly be visualised as coming to pass in this world, yet even in this world, we may occasionally come across such behaviour and gain hope from it for the future.

Let me give an example. A man came to Jesus, knelt before him, and asked him: 'Good teacher, what must I do to inherit eternal life?' Jesus answers simply in terms of the traditional law: 'You know the commandments: Do not kill, Do not commit adultery, Do not steal, Do not bear false witness. Do not defraud, Honour your father and mother.' The man replied: 'Teacher, all these I have observed from my youth.' We are told that Jesus looked on him and loved him and then added: 'You lack one thing; go, sell what you have and give to the poor, and you will have treasure in heaven: and come, follow me.' The gospel account continues: 'At that saying, his countenance fell, and he went away sorrowful: for he had great possessions' (Mark 10. 17–22).

What do we make of that story? I suppose if we agreed with Schweitzer, we could make sense of it, for if the world was going to end in a few months' time, this man might as well get rid of his fortune and gain merit in the coming kingdom. If we reject Schweitzer's idea, we can hardly suppose that this was a universal principle of morality that Jesus was putting forth. There would be complete chaos if *everybody* began to give away his or her possessions, and if they were given to the poor, would this not simply create a new group of rich people? But suppose we try the 'radical obedience' option and think that Jesus' words are addressed to a minority in society, and that their action makes present the kingdom of heaven here and now on earth, giving, as it were, flashes of a reality which lies beyond this world. This is in fact how the Church itself eventually began to interpret the really strenuous commands of Jesus. Of course, the idea that there is a 'religious life' with special demands and special standards is not a popular one at the present time and was never popular with Protestants. Yet perhaps it helps us to understand some of Jesus' teaching. In one of his parables, he teaches: 'The kingdom of heaven is like the leaven, which a woman took and hid in three measures of flour, till it was all leavened.' Here the suggestion seems to be that the kingdom is like the leaven rather than the whole loaf – at least, the kingdom so far as it is already present on this earth.

It may seem strange that when the notion of the kingdom of God plays such a prominent role in Jesus teaching about human conduct, it is so difficult to derive from that teaching very much in the way of a political or social theology. Jesus certainly recognised that every human being is also a social being. The social dimension is built into the very constitution of humanity. In the first chapter of Genesis, when God resolves to create man in his own image and likeness, he creates in fact a social unit, the first couple: 'Male and female created he them.' But most of Jesus' moral teaching is directed to moral agents in their individual or small-scale relations to one another. Two other very important concepts emerge in the course of the teaching, the concept of love and the concept of the neighbour. We have already noted that when Jesus summed up the law, he introduced the notion of love: 'Thou shalt love the Lord thy God with all thy heart and with all thy soul and with all thy mind and with all thy strength,' and:'Thou shalt love thy neighbour as thyself.' In saying this, Jesus was putting love above every other command of the law. Indeed, in the opinion of the American moralist Paul Ramsey, Jesus not only put love above the rest of the law but infinitely above. This means in effect that where there is any conflict of laws or rules, love must take precedence. We see this in Jesus' own activities, for instance, when he heals on the sabbath day (a work of love taking precedence over a traditional obligation).

Theologians have spent much time and energy analysing Christian love and have sometimes tried to show that it is of a unique kind and different from any other love. It so happens that in Greek the

New Testament uses a special word for love, *agape*, and this has encouraged the belief that this love is of a distinct kind. But I doubt very much that this is the case. Christian love does not differ fundamentally from natural loves such as family love or friendship. Once again, what Jesus has done is to deepen the traditional ideas and to give them a new seriousness, not to replace them with something quite new. His own love for the human race is surely the deepest love that has ever been known in this world, so that we recognise in it the very love of God himself.

If Christ has deepened the concept of love, surely through the concept of the neighbour he has given it a breadth that it never had before. We have seen that the Old Testament, too, commended the love of the neighbour. But, always, the neighbour was someone who had a certain claim upon you. He might be the person who lived next door or a member of the same tribe or community or religion. In this celebrated Parable of the Good Samaritan, Jesus swept away all such limitations. The neighbour is simply any human being whom you meet along life's way and who needs help and support. He may even be a member of what is counted as a hostile group. Here we do move into new territory where Jesus is indeed a moral pioneer.

The question may still be troubling us: 'Is not all this far beyond human strength, an impossible task?' I suppose we have to say, 'Yes, it is.' But in Christianity, as also in Judaism, morals are inseparable from religion. It is claimed that our human weakness is supplemented by divine grace, and that through prayer and the sacraments and hearing the scriptures, human beings are strengthened to face moral demands. It is true that we shall still fall, through negligence, through weakness, through our own deliberate fault. But many before us, who shared our weaknesses, have shown how much human life can be raised through following in the Christian way. 'Therefore, since we are surrounded by so great a cloud of witnesses, let us also lay aside every weight, and sin which clings so closely, and let us run with perseverance the race that is set before us, looking to Jesus.' (Hebrews 12. 1–2).

John Macquarrie, now retired, was formerly Lady Margaret Professor of Divinity in the University of Oxford and a Canon of Christ Church.

The legacy of the past

John Greenhalgh

IN MY YOUTH, one of the features of notice boards outside non-conformist chapels (and some churches) was the Wayside Pulpit, on which appeared pithy statements reminding passers-by of their destiny and responsibilities as children of God. My favourite was this gem: 'Your place in the hereafter depends on what you're after here!' The message is that behaviour counts, indeed is of vital importance, of eternal significance. And, by implication, can be informed by the gospel of Jesus Christ.

Whatever the ultimate nature of the universe God has created, it is certainly a *moral* universe. It is axiomatic, also, that, as the Wayside Pulpit so vividly informs us, the present will affect the future as much as what has happened in the past affects our present judgement of the ethical basis for our existence. But, how far in the past do we need to go, the better to understand the present? And, what exactly is it, in the present, that needs to be understood as we face the future?

To take the second question first, in the world around us we encounter behaviour that, were it not so horribly a part of reality, would be literally, unimaginable in the sense that we *cannot* imagine, say, Central London being vaporised in an atomic explosion. Consider what is permitted, by different cultures, to happen both to human beings and to the natural world of which humanity is a part. Public opinion tolerates the torture and maiming and sexual abuse of women and men for political ends. It denies human rights. It annihilates civilian communities in Nagasaki or Dresden in the name of war. It accepts the existence of children living in sewers or turning to prostitution: it sends them to clear mine fields and exploits them in factories. It encourages the killing of human life in abortion. It practises genocide on Jews, on Biafrans, and 'racial cleansing'. Ultimately, there is a moral dilemma which faces mankind: it does not respect human nature any more then it respects the natural world of which it is a part. The rain forests, the ozone layer and the whale are but the latest victims of man's rape of nature.

How can this be? St Paul faced the same dilemma of understanding when he wrote in Romans 1.29–31:

They were filled with all manner of wickedness, evil, covetousness, malice. Full of envy, murder, strife, deceit, malignity. They are gossips, slanderers, haters of God, insolent, haughty, boastful, inventors of evil, disobedient to parents, foolish, faithless, heartless, ruthless.

The Church's subsequent theological definition 'original sin' is not a bad way of summarising what Paul was describing in the Roman Empire or we can describe equally vividly in our own, often bestial, world today.

There is another issue which needs to be raised at this juncture. It is frequently stated as a truism that the moral standards and values of society at large change from age to age but that Christian gospel values do not, that they are as true and relevant for us now as they were 2000 years ago. But is this really the case? Does not Christianity accommodate the world in which it exists? Is Christianity *par excellence* the most syncretistic of all religions? Or the least?

The moral standards of our own society in Britain allow a great number of things which are sub-Christian. What does the Supreme Governor of the established Church of England think when she gives the Royal Assent to a bill legalising scientific experiments on a foetus? Her coronation oath? Will she be as compliant towards future legislation on euthanasia? Is she, though, in the trap of the double standard of private *versus* public conscience and responsibility? For don't we all have to ask, as Norry McCurry and David Alton do in their articles in this book, 'Where do I stand?' – at some point in life? This may take many forms. Two of the most common are whether to condone adultery or to fight in a war, either as a party involved or by associations of friendship or patriotism.

Thus we return to our original questions: what factors make some things acceptable to us and not others; how far back do we need to go to assess the influences on our society inherited from previous generations? On a theological level we need to go right back to the aetiological stories in the early chapters of the Bible where many of the problems that beset our society today are presented in Genesis as myths of pre-history: to the Garden of Eden (for deception and disobedience), to Cain and Abel (for the wilful killing of one's own species), or to the Tower of Babel (for the breakdown of a political consensus).

Consider this post-diluvian statement addressed to mankind from the pen of the Elohist writer of Genesis 9.2: 'The fear of you and the dread of you shall fall on all animals on earth, on all birds of heaven, on everything that moves upon the ground, and all fish in the sea.' The key words are 'fear' (*mora'kem*) and 'dread' (*chitkem*): they do not occur in the Creation narrative of Genesis 1. How terrifying that man has become opposed to, stands against that very nature of which he is a part. It is indeed a fallen world that we live in. At this stage reference must be made to the implications of the *linear* view of time (which is western and Christian) as opposed to the *cyclical* view of time (which is eastern). The cyclical view is very seductive. It places man more in harmony with nature. It also makes it easier, if reincarnation is a reality, to come to terms with the tragedy of a life cut short by illness, accident, disease or the evil of man. A belief in the immortality of the soul, which is part of Christian thinking, quickly absorbs, on the level of folk religion, the attendant doctrine of the transmigration of souls. It even surfaced in the scholarly apologetics of the great third-century theologian, Origen. But, in doctrinal theology as in moral theology, there is a point beyond which syncretism is not possible without a denial of the gospel. The linear view of history is possibly harder to live with than the cyclical, but equally the virtues of faith, hope and love are harder to live by than the pagan, cardinal ones of fortitude, prudence, justice and temperance.

As Christians our understanding and awareness of the morality of God must be based on two complementary and inter-related theologies: the doctrines of creation and of the paschal mystery. To these Brian Horne and Nicholas Kavanagh address themselves in their essays in this book. Our concern here is to ask what developments in recent time, from an historian's perspective, have played a part in influencing our thinking about ethical values in the spheres of science, demographic theory and nationalism, economics and philosophy.

Science

THE SO-NAMED 'scientific' revolution began in the seventeenth century. Some of the great thinkers, then and later, are household names: Francis Bacon, Galileo Galilei, Isaac Newton, Charles Darwin, Albert Einstein, Stephen Hawking. Their achievements in the realm of science have been colossal, but what has been the result of these achievements on our moral perspectives?

Essentially, what scientists have done collectively has been to remove that fundamental element of 'mystery' from life, and thus to subject everything in nature to the combined dictates of reason and experiment in order to formulate scientific laws which in their turn appear to offer a sufficiency that would have been rejected by the European mind of an earlier age. What happened was that 'scientific' knowledge came to have nothing to do with (moral and other) **values**, nor on a more instinctual level with **intuition**. Technology was soon to reign supreme; nature was exploited; religion and science were understood, wrongly, to have, in modern jargon, separate agendas.

What was utterly destroyed was the biblical unity where man was able to relate, within the natural world, to God. Now, in the late-twentieth century, man is encouraged to relate, through the natural world, only to himself. He has become anthropocentric in his vision of life and style of living; worst of all, in a very real sense, he is destroying that natural world of which he is a constituent part. We are soon back to the book of Genesis. Mankind has set himself up as a god. The scientific idol is the machine, whether the obvious motor car that replaces sabbath worship or those mechanistic processes that de-personalise humanity, from *in vitro* fertilisation onwards through life. Truly, men now believe they are in control of their own destinies. Scientists have forgotten eternity. We must not do so. We are back not only to Genesis but to the Wayside Pulpit.

There is an irony here. Scientists frequently exhibit characteristics of withdrawal from the world they explore, lead exemplary lives, and have a deep-seated respect for the very things they subject to examination and formulation. But, the modern scientist's end is not the discovery of God, only the discovery, and frequently the appropriation, of His created universe. By contrast theology's concerns are a far cry from those of modern science which does not teach the **Way** (how to live), the **Truth** (what to believe), and the **Life** (the reward of eternal life to be experienced now).

We all want to know what is the reality of existence and the explanation of human life. But the danger of the scientific revolution is this: the supposition that the answers to these questions, like those of quantum mechanics, can be obtained through the laws of physics, for these laws do not allow us, in their rigid and impersonal approach, to speak in terms of **values**, whether emotional, gospel or moral.

Demographic theory and nationalism

THOMAS MALTHUS, in his *Essay on Population*, said that while food supplies tended to increase in an arithmetic ratio (1–2–3–4–5–6), population growth increased geometrically (1–2–4–8–16–32). It was obvious that there had to be natural restraints on the growth of population if it were to be fed. These restraints, Malthus argued, were natural and threefold: war, famine and disease (in a later edition, Malthus added a fourth: moral restraint).

The present Pope and his predecessor, Paul VI, have made their voices heard, to little acclaim, on the subject of moral restraint; meanwhile, there has been a tacit acceptance in the 200 years since Malthus published his *Essay* that the human race has, almost of necessity, to live with war, famine and disease, and that, in spite of pacifism, aid and medicine, people are going to fight, crops to fail and plagues to visit us. The Second World War claimed 60 million lives, the drought in Africa and elsewhere since 1945 has resulted in even more deaths, and AIDS may yet prove to be the numerical winner with the scythe.

This has all affected our vision of people, their importance, their freedom and potential. The Four Horsemen of the Apocalypse, it may be argued, are nothing new, but during the 200 years since the birth of Malthusianism new meanings for old words have entered our dictionaries: words such as holocaust, concentration camp, and conscription. They have all evolved and been used against a background of nationalistic growth.

The Old Testament has much to say about nationalism. Yahweh's chosen people, the Jews, are contrasted with the 'nations' (or gentiles: the words are synonymous). For Israel is not a nation state, but a theocracy. Its ruler is God. The low spot of the Old Testament is, in many senses, *not* the Enslavement in Egypt, nor the Exile in Babylon, nor the Fall of Jerusalem, but the events recorded in 1 Samuel when the people came to Samuel and said 'appoint us a king to govern us, like other nations' (1 Samuel 8.5). This is apostasy: 'It is I whom they have rejected, I whom they will not have to be their king' as Yahweh says (1 Samuel 8.7); it is also idolatory.

What of the 'terror' bombing of Wurzburg, Hildesheim and Rothenburg in March, 1945, a few weeks before the end of the war, in which the victims were women and children? It is the ability to *accept* these acts for reasons of state (*pace* Bishop Bell) even if there is total personal disapproval of the acts themselves that is the legacy of nationalism in our time.

The beginnings of nationalism in England are very early, antedating the establishment of the Tudor dynasty, but in central and eastern Europe nationalism is a nineteenth- and twentieth-century phenomenon (later in time because of the persistence of imperial ambitions of Germans, Franks, Russians and Turks). The emergent nation states inherited the low, Malthusian view of humanity. Conscription is the symbol of the nation state's usurpation of personal freedom and the subjection of men's minds in preparation for the horrors we have considered. Conscription is the modern press gang at work, curtailing the liberty and dignity of human beings. Yet, it is accepted because of a *credo* of a different kind: *Dulce et decorum est pro patria mori*. The restricted conscription of earlier days (e.g. during the English Civil War) was very different from the modern, universal form.

Modern nation states, in the demands they have laid on their citizens, have radically affected the vision of how we can and should behave. Samuel warned the people of Israel against nationalism 3000 years ago. The consequences then may be read in 1 Samuel 8.11–17. The story is the same: unbridled nationalism leads to totalitarianism and a loss of respect for the individual. How this pattern in recent history has affected eastern Europe is the subject of Hugh Wybrew's article in this book.

Economics

THE THEME of exploitation and loss of personal freedom may be continued in examining the economic practices associated with the industrial revolution. Indeed, nowhere is the loss of control over our own individual destiny seen more clearly than in the 'rise' of capitalism. Capitalism is, in fact, as old as mankind. It begins when man starts to produce or to acquire, and then to store, more than he needs for his daily wants. In its wake it brings inequality and opportunism. The animal may be judged much wiser. As D. H. Lawrence puts it in a pertinent, witty and moving short *Pansy*:

> The mosquito knows full well, small as he is
> he's a beast of prey.
> But after all
> he only takes his bellyful,
> he doesn't put my blood in the bank.

But capitalism may also offer a road to posterity and a path of progress as well as the exercise of power and privilege and usury. The commercial revolutions of the sixteenth and seventeenth centuries led to the industrial revolutions of the nineteenth and twentieth. They were capitalistic enterprises, indeed the former financed the latter, and, during the course of their growth and development, something very significant happened. In terms of economic theory it may be stated very simply: instead of man controlling the factors of production, he himself became one of them, in the hands of the entrepreneur.

The slow transformation from a rural village division of labour, to manufacture in a domestic workshop, to the factory system was slow for some, dramatic for others. It took place against a background of the mechanising and reorganisation of agriculture and brought in its wake an organised labour movement, a complex banking system, primitive arrangements for poor relief, and a spur to invention.

What did it do to Man? In short, there was a dehumanising process where independence of action was progressively removed from him. The industrial worker of the eighteenth and nineteenth centuries was put either underground or in a factory and rewarded in monetary terms against an unpredictable trade cycle of supply and demand over which he had no control. His predecessor, the fifteenth-century farm worker could gather wood, season it and build a table. The same worker in the twentieth century has to place himself in the control of an employer and earn money in order to buy or make himself the same table. In one sense, it may be argued, it is no different from the labourers in the vineyard who rented themselves out for a penny a day, but of course it is – not in terms of putative capitalism, but in terms of the personal relationships enjoyed by all.

We return, as before, to the individual's relationship to others and to his vision of himself. What he is allowed to be and to become is deeply affected by modern economic (and thus political) thinking. Mrs Thatcher's *guru*, the remarkable Friedrich von Hayek, who died in March, 1992, made numerous detailed and careful examinations of the relationship of the individual to the state, in economic terms as well as political. For Hayek the two were inextricably linked. His name ranks with Keynes and Beveridge among those who have influenced the thinking of British governments in this century. He spoke out against a state that placed limitations on the freedom of the individual. He attacked the (socialist) vision of a controlled society. He believed (and has been proved right) that any form of collectivism was doomed to failure.

So, again, it looks simple: the socialistic 'doctrines' of the re-distribution of wealth and state intervention and control, both militate against personal freedom and must be rejected in favour of free enterprise. But, can it ever be *so* simple? Do we need the prophetic voice of the Christian Church, informing the mind of the state? The dark side of the capitalistic coin undoubtedly accommodates things which are not acceptable, which are anti-gospel. Exploitation is no answer to the stranglehold formerly exercised by organised labour. Market forces should not be allowed to make innocent victims of working people. Homelessness and the degradation experienced by the beggars on our streets are not acceptable options for state hand-outs. The labourer *is* worthy of his hire; there *must* be an 'option for the poor' written in to the morality of society.

At root all this is a way of looking at humanity, to which we have accustomed ourselves, which has been made acceptable by the economic legacies of the past.

Philosophy

IT IS HARDLY possible to over-estimate the impact of the writings of Emmanuel Kant, who lived from 1724 to 1804. In a very real sense, Kant moved the goal posts by suggesting that God is not an *objective* reality; by implication he also opened the door to the suggestion that there is no *objective* morality. If our vision of God is relative, so will be our moral standards.

Kantian philosophy is thus anthropocentric, like modern science. The central ideas of religion – God himself, free will, immortality – are not revealed *to* man but understood *by* man. So, in Kantian terms, there is no vision of God transcendent. There is no need for the traditional 'proofs' for the existence of God (the ontological, the teleological, the cosmological): our inherited notions about God are to be rejected because they are not part of our own experience of him. We need no longer personify God (or the Devil) any more than we might personify Nemesis in a platonic sense or Wisdom in a hellenistic sense.

Can we truly live with this? For Kant, and us, in a real sense, it doesn't matter, because we are still seeing the same, transcendent God, albeit differently. But there is an alternative response: we do without God altogether. And it is this response that has been made by many, many people in the West in our so-called post-Christian, post-Kantian age. We do not need his objectivity to understand God or to explain our subjective relationship to him.

Within this framework of religious thinking, scientific rationalism slots in very neatly. Let us consider a few practical examples which demonstrate the marginalising of God in our lives. A woman wants a baby and cannot conceive; she is unlikely to confine herself to prayer as Hannah did in the temple at Shiloh: rather her doctor prescribes a pill to stimulate her pituitary gland. A man with a sore throat on February 3rd will consider it more practical to pay a visit to the ENT specialist at his local hospital than seek blessed candles and the intercession of St Blaise. The parents of a child with a galloping pneumonic, non-viral infection turn to antibiotics rather than the relic of a saint for recovery. Equally, the woman troubled in marriage no longer prays to the bearded St Uncumber nor the man to St Jude. They turn elsewhere.

This marginalising of God has had a profound effect on our moral conduct. A relative ethic has replaced an absolute one. Morals and values, like God, have become a matter for the individual to decide upon. There is everywhere a rejection of any *magisterium*. We may observe a similar process in other areas of life. Obedience is to the self. Our faith lies in our own ability to make the rules of right conduct for ourselves. The inevitable result has been a kind of moral confusion. But do we return to the old absolutes? Canon Pilkington's article has much to say about this.

Living without God?

OUR TOLERANCE of wickedness is the result of the climate of opinion of our age, our legacy from the past, and it is reflected in the laws of our land. We do not burn witches today but we do abort foetuses (and if we live in China, permit infanticide – of girls, of course); we do not cast out sodomites but we have turned our backs on the sanctity of marriage. What does this imply? That witchcraft and sodomy don't matter? Certainly, neither the unborn child nor the nuptial vows have any meaningful status in law in our society.

The way we have come to look at the world, scientifically, economically, politically and philosophically, has resulted in the changing of the bases of our ethical values. Mankind's vision of itself and what it should be is in confusion. The essays in this book suggest a return to gospel values. We may be forced, most of the time, with a choice between the lesser of two evils, but our principles must be sound. Pope Paul VI's great battle cry was *La vita umana è sacra*. Our task is to consider how to recapture a vision of the essential holiness of Man, beyond the legacy of the immediate past, and inform our consciences in readiness for the difficult moral choices we will be called upon to make. Let us remember one thing. We need never take the devil as an example for what we do.

John Greenhalgh is verger and lay administrator at St Mary's, Bourne Street.

On the theology of creation

Brian Horne

It is in the sacramental view of the universe, both of its material and its spiritual elements, that there is given hope of making human both politics and economics and of making effectual both faith and love.[1]

IN HIS most recent study of the relationship between science and religion, *Cosmos and Creator*, Stanley L. Jaki remarks that 'the theology of creation has been for many decades a stepchild in comparison with a large number of theological topics centring mostly on the notion of the church.'[2] Jaki is thinking of the shifts of theological interest during the twentieth century; but it is not as though the theology of creation previously occupied a prominent place in the family of Christian teachings which has now been taken by more legitimate claimants. 'Creation' has seldom been at the centre of theological discussion at any time in the history of the Church; it has, in a sense, always been a stepchild. The doctrine stands as an assertion in the opening words of the Bible: 'In the beginning God created . . .' and as the first article of belief in the Christian creed: 'I believe in God the Father almighty, maker of heaven and earth . . .'; but compared to the vast literature of interpretation which surrounds the other major affirmations of the Christian religion that which accompanies creation is relatively meagre. The great controversies of Christian theology have revolved around other issues, the person of Christ, the Trinity, the Church, sin and grace: the notion of creation has been assumed and accepted rather than discussed and defined. There is even some debate about the propriety of treating the doctrine of creation as though it were a major theological issue.

In his commentary on *Genesis* Gerhard Von Rad illustrates one side of that debate when he suggests that:

The position of the creation story at the beginning of our Bible has often led to misunderstanding, as though the 'doctrine' of creation were a central subject of Old Testament faith . . . Rather the position of both the Yahwist and the Priestly documents is basically faith in salvation and election. They undergirded this faith by the testimony that this Yahweh, who made a covenant with Abraham and at Sinai, is also the creator of the world. Therefore, with all its astonishing concentration on the individual aspects of its faith in creation, this preface has only an ancillary function.[3]

Stanley Jaki, on the other hand, maintains that the first chapter of *Genesis* (however its details may be interpreted) 'stands in front of all books of biblical revelation as a warning that the salvation to be achieved through revelation rests on the dogma of creation.'[4]

When one looks at the history of the Church it would seem, on the surface at least, that the theological emphasis of the Jewish religion, as identified by Von Rad, is that which has been favoured also in the Christian tradition – at least in the West. The classical dogmatic formulation of the theology of creation, 'creatio ex nihilo', was only incorporated into the official teaching of the Latin Church as late as the Fourth Lateran Council in 1215. We shall dwell on this briefly as the reasons for its promulgation at this precise moment in history help to illustrate the way in which particular aspects of Christian belief attract particular attention at particular times. There had emerged in northern Italy and southern France during the twelfth century a heretical Christian sect centred on the city of Albi. It was the most recent and most powerful manifestation of that 'philosophical' movement and way of life known as Gnosticism. Gnosticism took (and still takes, for it is by no means extinct) many forms, but at the heart of most of these forms is a doctrine of radical dualism i.e. a belief about the unbridgeable gap between matter and spirit, a fundamental separation between body and soul. Such a dualism regards the universe, the material of the created order as inherently evil and the world of the senses a perilous place. The existence of this world in which individual spirits are unhappily imprisoned can only be explained by supposing that it was the work of a supernatural and malevolent force eternally opposed to a God whose nature being essentially spiritual and immaterial, was above and beyond all contact with matter. The implications for Christianity were (and are) obvious: the Incarnation becomes an impossibility, the utterly spiritual God could not have been contaminated by the flesh of the earthly Jesus; the Church with its sacramental use of matter and involvement with the life of society was to be rejected for a purely spiritual religion in which the desires of the body would often be harshly suppressed; and, of course, God could not have been responsible for a world which might, as far as anyone could tell, have always been in existence as something totally alien to him.

Since her very beginnings the Christian Church has always had to confront the dualistic tendencies of the human mind; and it responded to the growth of Catharism in the twelfth century in France and Italy with ferocious persecution: the Albigensian crusade. But, in addition to this terrible physical suppression, there was also an attempt to persuade by argument and teaching, and out of this came the promulgation by the Fourth Lateran Council of the dogma of 'creatio ex nihilo'.[5] It declared in unequivocal language that God alone, the Father of the Lord Jesus Christ, was the source of all that existed; that in His absolute power and freedom He chose to bring the universe into being 'out of nothing'. There was no equally powerful contrary force, matter was not eternal nor was it evil. Creation was an activity of a loving God that was both 'new' and good. Evil, even if one did acknowledge the existence of Satan, lay not in stuff of the universe but in the perverse tendencies of the human will.

This doctrine of creation 'out of nothing' had been a fully articulated part of Jewish belief since the second century BC and was accepted, though not much discussed, by the majority of Christian teachers from the beginning of the Christian era; but it was the particular circumstances of the late twelfth century which concentrated the mind of the Church on this particular aspect of her faith and forced her to bring to the intellectual battle against Catharism an ancient formula: 'creatio ex nihilo'. What is important to notice is the fact that the making of doctrine is, frequently, not the result of calm, disinterested speculation by religious geniuses remote from the turbulence of everyday life, but arises out of necessity in specific historical situations. This does not mean that the formulation has relevance only in the situation for which it was designed, but it is as well to be clear about what forces operate when theology is being constructed.

In succeeding centuries attention moved away from ideas of creation into other aspects of the faith; and the theology of creation remained a peripheral issue until the rise of the natural sciences once again compelled the Church to come to terms with developments in perceptions of the world that seemed to offer a challenge to Christian perspectives. What eighteenth and nineteenth century theologians had to face was a world which scientists and philosophers had, apparently, successfully desacralised: the 'coincidence' of the natural and supernatural which was an integral part of both Patristic and medieval belief had disappeared. This separation of the natural and the supernatural orders made possible both the advances in western European science and also the alienation of man from Nature.

Now, more than ever, there is needed a reconsideration and, possibly re-interpretation or recovery, of a Christian theology of creation. I am not proposing anything like the promulgation of dogmatic formulae, only the urgent need for serious study and convincing theological exposition. The compulsion arises now not out of the need to combat a Christian heresy, nor even the need to counter what many supposed was the 'atheism' of science, but out of the urgent need of the Church to say something morally and spiritually meaningful in the context of the human race's increasing anxiety about its problematic relationship with Nature. In the face of contemporary realities like the possibility of extinction by nuclear warfare, the ecological crisis and the environmental destruction in many parts of the world, it seems unreal to speak about salvation as though it were a doctrine purely about human redemption and unconnected with the integrity of the whole of creation. We are beginning to see deeper and wider implications of St Paul's words:

For the creation waits with eager longing for the revealing of the sons of God . . . because the creation itself will be set free from its bondage to decay and obtain the glorious liberty of the children of God. We know that the whole creation has been groaning in travail until now.[6]

It is the pressure of environmental issues which is compelling the Church as never before to recognise that a doctrine of God as creator and lover of the world implies the necessity of living in that world – and being responsible for that world – in such a way that the attitudes of society as a whole to the question of man's relationship with nature will be transformed. If there is to be a halt to the destruction of our environment then a change must begin at a fundamental level. Human beings are not, as the Gnostics would have us believe, souls to be plucked out of matter on the day of salvation; we are, as is suggested by St Paul, part of a universe which waits for a consummation that has been promised by God in Christ. The doctrines of salvation, the Church, even the doctrines of the Incarnation and the Trinity, are having to re-locate themselves within a theology of Creation.

It would be wrong of me to give the impression that questions like: *What does it mean to say that God 'creates'? What kind of world has been, and is being, created? What is the place and function of the human species in this created order? What is the purpose and goal of the universe?* have been ignored by the great Christian thinkers of the past. They have not. Because of the essential integrity of all Christian doctrine it is impossible to expound belief about God, Christ and the Church without addressing creation, but there was, inevitably, a sense in which creation was always interpreted in the light of what one said about these, apparently prior, doctrines. What I am suggesting is a shifting perspective: these doctrines being reconsidered in the light of a theology of creation. And it is here that the spiritual and theological approaches of Anglicanism and eastern Orthodoxy may have something special to contribute to the debate, for both traditions have kept alive certain issues which traditional Catholicism and Protestantism have tended to treat perfunctorily.

I have prefaced this essay with a quotation taken from William Temple, Archbishop of Canterbury from 1942 to 1944. In 1934 he published his Gifford lectures under the title *Nature, Man and God*, a book which, despite its faults, was quickly recognised as a classical exposition of a certain kind of Anglican theology. The argument of the book reaches its climax in the nineteenth lecture which Temple called *The Sacramental Universe*. All the earlier discussions about Personality, Revelation, History have been leading to this: the perception of the universe as 'sacramental', of the natural world (both human and non-human) as the place in which and by which the personal God is encountered and revealed. 'It is to such a view that our whole course of enquiry has been leading us; and it is such a view which affords the strongest hope for the continuance in reality and power of religious faith and practice.'[7] It is precisely this concept of the sacramental universe that the Christian Church needs to recover and preach now if its voice is going to be heard in the debates about the future of our planet. It is this concept that I should like to lay at the foundation of a theology of creation. It is, perhaps, by means of this that a renewed understanding of the relationship between the natural and the supernatural may be reached.

Again, I am not suggesting that the concept is a new one: it is implicit in such diverse thinkers as Irenaeus (130–200), Augustine of Hippo (354–430), Thomas Aquinas (1225–1274) and John Calvin (1509–1564)[8] but it has seldom achieved so central and powerful a position in a systematic theology as in Temple's. 'In nature we find God; we do not only infer from Nature what God must be like, but when we see Nature truly, we see God self-manifested in and through it.' So far, so good; none of the thinkers previously mentioned would have found any cause for disagreement with that; it is when Temple goes further to talk of the way in which the revelation of God in nature occurs that he parts company with the Augustianism of Catholicism and the Calvinism of Protestantism.

We affirm, then, that unless all our existence is a medium of revelation, no particular revelation is possible . . . Only if God is revealed in the rising of the sun in the sky can he be revealed in the rising of a son of man from the dead . . . only if nothing is profane can anything be sacred.[9]

What, if I am not mistaken, is being argued here is not only that the created order and human flesh have been 'graced' by the incarnation of the divine Word in Jesus Christ, but that creation was always 'graced' and has, despite evil and corruption, remained 'graced' from the beginning.

What we have here is the total rejection of any form of dualism; and I should like to spell out some of its implications for belief and behaviour. First, God must, in some way, be responsible for evil as well as good. There can be no moment in history, no occurrence in the universe, when he has been absent; he may be present only in the forms of deliberate powerlessness, but present he must be. Secondly, it cannot be by escaping from the world of matter that He is found: a religion which believes that it is only by contemplation that the divine can be reached is not the Christian religion. Even the most rigorous of the self-denying mystics of the Egyptian deserts accepted the absolute necessity of the sacraments of baptism and the eucharist. Thirdly, it means that the primary, perhaps the only proper, attitude of the human species to the world it inhabits is one of reverence, and that within that reverence the humble wish to 'fit in' with as well as 'control' nature. This reverence does not preclude intellectual curiosity or, even, experimentation, but it does forbid the exploitation and abuse of nature. Fourthly, there can be no such thing as ownership. In the ultimate sense no-one can own anything; there may be ownership in a *derived* sense, but ultimately everything belongs to God and what he 'owns' is the universe which He has freely and deliberately made as sacramental of Himself. This last point is frequently spoken of but seldom taken seriously. Very few people ask themselves: 'What is the purpose, the ultimate purpose, for which I own this thing? What is *its* ultimate purpose?' The sense that everything exists only to glorify God seldom enters into consideration when one 'acquires' a house or a piece of land – or a bottle of wine. But if human beings really understand their role as the 'agents' of creation, the enablers of all things in the natural order to achieve their proper end, it might radically alter our attitude to the use of natural resources.

I hope I have not given the impression that Temple was presenting a cleverly-disguised kind of Nature worship. Such was certainly not the case: the emphasis on the *sacramental* character of the world disbars that. Moreover he was concerned to emphasise that the self-revelation of God in Nature was not complete. He wrote:

Personality can only reveal itself in persons. Consequentially it is specially in human nature . . . that we see God. But human nature is a thing self-confessedly defective; whether still struggling to its self-realisation, or fallen from an 'original righteousness', it can give but a fitful and distorted representation of the personal reality from which it springs. If in the midst of the world-process there should occur an instance of human nature free from blemish or defect, there might be found there the perfect self-expression of God to those who share that human nature.[10]

He is referring, somewhat obliquely, to the incarnation. I should like to extend Temple's argument here further than he might have thought proper and in a vocabulary which did not occur to him, but which seems to be a natural corollary of his own: the incarnate Lord himself can be described as sacrament. In a sacramental universe Christ is to be seen both as the supreme and as the unique sacrament of God. He not only reveals the Father, He reveals the Father in a particular manner: the manner of a sacrament which acts as a sign embodying in itself the reality it is representing. In a sacramental universe we must expect the ultimate revelation of God to take the form of a human person. The world of nature is as much the explanation of the appearance of Christ as he is the means of its redemption. Considered historically, the incarnation is already implicit in creation: the creative process begun 'ex nihilo' only reveals its true purpose in the divinisation of human nature by the act in which the divine word appears in history as a human being. And with this joining of the natural and the supernatural in Christ goes the possibility of the sanctification of the whole world.

Earlier, I used, in trying to identify the function of human beings in relation to the rest of nature, the terms 'agents' and 'enablers'; and I should like briefly to amplify what I then said. In the seventh century Leontios of Neapolis described this relationship picturesquely:

The creation does not venerate the Creator through itself directly, but it is through me that the heavens declare the glory of God, through me the moon offers him homage, through me the stars ascribe glory to him, through me the waters, rain and dew worship and glorify him.[11]

This perception is based upon the notion (already present in much Patristic theology) that man is the microcosm of creation. This notion that in humanity all of the rest of nature is 'gathered' may seem, at first, arrogant; in fact, it is just the opposite for it compels the human race to recognise its responsibility towards the rest of nature.

It even reverses the normal western perception that the world exists for the sake of the human race; instead – and paradoxically, because the human species is the most powerful – humanity is seen as existing for the sake of nature. It is only when human beings begin to achieve sanctification i.e. living the life of God, that the whole natural order can begin to enter its own destiny in God. This has been a theme of the theology of creation in much Eastern Orthodox thinking.

Man no longer saves himself through the universe, but the universe is saved through man. For man is the hypostasis of the whole cosmos which participates in his nature . . . To the universe, man is the hope of receiving grace and unity with God, and also the danger of failure and fallenness'.[12]

So the terms used earlier – agents and enablers – are not adequate, not strong enough, to bear the meaning of this relationship we are identifying. The term we need is 'priest' – the human race exercises a priestly function towards the whole created order.

At this point, too, the theology of creation joins with and passes into the theology of the Church. If all that has, so far, been said is true, the Church cannot merely be seen as the company of the faithful in which the word of the gospel is preached and received by those who have heard the call to discipleship of Christ; nor the body of Christians in which individual souls are fed and sanctified by the sacramental food of the eucharist. A much larger vision is needed in which it will be perceived that in eucharistic worship begins the process of establishing the correct relationship of humanity with the world and also the drawing of that world into the share of the sanctifying grace of God. At the Offertory in the eucharist of the Alternative Services Book of the Church of England a prayer (drawn from 1 Chronicles 29.11) is suggested:

Yours, Lord, is the greatness, the power, the glory, the splendour, and the majesty; for everything in heaven and on earth is yours. All things come from you, and of your own do we give you.

The bread and wine are presented at the altar to symbolise the offering of the whole of the material, natural world by man in his capacity as priest of that world. 'Thus, humanity, as the priestly microcosm, assumes a stance of mediator as well as king over the material creation.'[13] It is in the light of these theological propositions that we need to order our lives and direct our actions.

Brian Horne is a lecturer at King's College, London, and an honorary assistant priest at St Mary's, Bourne Street. This article is based on material produced by him for the Archbishops' Commission on Rural Areas.

Notes

1. William Temple *Nature, Man and God* (Macmillan, 1934)
2. Stanley L. Jaki. *Cosmos and Creator*. (Scottish Academic Press, 1980) p. 85
3. Gerhard Von Rad. *Genesis* (Westminster Press) p. 45
4. *op. cit*. p. 64
5. 'We firmly believe and plainly confess that the true God is One . . . who through his omnipotent power created out of nothing at the beginning of time simultaneously both creatures, spiritual and corporeal, that is, angelic and of this world.'
6. Romans 8.19–22
7. *op. cit*. p. 486
8. 'It is only where God speaks and awakens human faith that the natural objects become sacramental. But this can happen to material things only because this is a sacramental universe, because God created all things visible and invisible.' *Institutes IV. XIV.* 18
9. *op. cit*. p. 306
10. *op. cit*. p. 266
11. See Kallistos Ware 'The Value of the Material World', *Sobornost*, series 6, no. 3 (1971)
12. V. Lossky *Orthodox Theology: an Introduction* translated by Kesarcadi-Watson (St Vladimir's Seminary Press, 1978) p. 71
13. See Stanley S. Harakas 'The Integrity of Creation and Ethics', *St Vladimir's Theological Quarterly*, vol. 32. no. 1 (1988) pp. 34–35

The paschal mystery and the question of meaning

Nicholas Kavanagh

Resurrection

IN HIS RECENT NOVEL, *On the Third Day,* Piers Paul Read describes
the consequences for a group of people of the supposed discovery
of the bones of Jesus of Nazareth in Jerusalem. For one character,
a high-flying young priest in the Vatican Curia, the discovery precipi-
tates a crisis of faith in which he renounces his beliefs, resigns his
orders and embarks on an extra-marital affair with an attractive
young woman. However improbable the plot of the novel, what the
author intends by this episode is, presumably, to show the close
connection between belief and morality and, for Christians at least,
the intimate connection between the bodily resurrection of Jesus and
the traditional Christian attitudes to sex. Not for this author the
sophisticated theological approaches of some contemporary thinkers,
in which the truth of the resurrection can somehow be preserved
irrespective of the fate of Jesus' mortal remains: rather, if God has
shown himself indifferent to the fate of Jesus' body, he is by implication indifferent to what we do with our own.

However uncompromising or unfashionable such an attitude may
be, it cannot be denied that it finds striking confirmation within
the earliest apostolic preaching. The apostle Paul, writing to the
Corinthians, is at great pains to stress the centrality and the fundamental nature of this event to the entire enterprise of faith, and –
by extension – faithful living (what he calls elsewhere 'the obedience
of faith'):

If Christ has not been raised, then our preaching is in vain and your faith
is in vain. We are even found to be misrepresenting God, because we
testified of God that he raised Christ, whom he did not raise if it is true

there is no resurrection of the dead. If Christ has not been raised then your faith is futile and you are still in your sins. Then those also who have fallen asleep in Christ have perished. If for this life only we have hope in Christ, we are of all men most to be pitied.[1]

Although addressed in the first instance to a small group of believers in the '50s AD, the claim for universal significance in the resurrection of Christ should not escape us. Involved in this is the fate of those believers who are dead as well as the present status of believers as freed from their sins and their future destiny. Past, present and future are all affected, as well as fundamental truth about God himself. 'Vain' and 'futile' are the words used to describe the reality of things if Christ has not been raised, a situation which we could speak of as aimless, purposeless, meaningless, condemned to frustration.

Leaving aside for the moment the question of whether the apostle is right to make the meaningfulness or otherwise of things dependent on the truth of the resurrection, it is obviously the case that a meaningless or pointless world renders any discussion of right and wrong, or morality, simply incoherent. Douglas Adams in his *Hitchhiker's Guide to the Galaxy* pokes gentle fun at the quest for 'The Meaning of Life, the Universe and Everything' (*What's the Answer? What exactly was the question?*) and many members of the academic and scientific establishments assure us that the fundamental questions that man has asked about himself, the world around him of which he is a part, his origin and destiny, are in fact meaningless and incoherent. (It is interesting, however, that this scepticism is usually reserved for the question of God, and rarely extends to the sceptics' own disciplines!)

Judgement

THE TRUTH is that human beings do not exist in a vacuum, and cannot live without a system of values to which they will ascribe meaning of a fundamental kind, and which they will use to make judgements and choices. If the value system is not grounded in a particular religious adherence, it will for the most part simply be absorbed uncritically from the surrounding culture, or climate of opinion.

Where that culture has radically separated itself from its roots in religious observance, the questions about ultimate meaning and value will be consciously or otherwise suppressed, and there will grow up powerful vested interests (economic, scientific, etc) to keep them suppressed. The North Atlantic culture in which we live has been compared to a giant conglomerate called Unbelievers and Consumers Incorporated whose business is fuelled by the fear of meaninglessness, by a profound sense of cosmic futility, and whose success depends on being able to persuade its shareholders and employees that this fear and anxiety can be allayed by an ever greater consumption of its products. It matters not that these products are raw materials, manufactured items, or people; what matters to the continuing success of the enterprise is that we find our system of values within it, that we accord it that ultimate significance which mankind calls *worship* (ascribing ultimate worth to it). There is, of course, nothing new in this: it is a description of the world under the control of the 'powers and principalities of this age', a situation exemplified in Revelation 18.11–13, in which human persons – the basis of Babylon's culture and economy – are at the bottom of the value scale.

If the foregoing appears as a call to a return to Victorian values or traditional concepts of morality, this would be a mistake: denunciation of the symptoms is all too easy (usually someone else's). Recently, a senior minister in the government blamed the Church for not preaching enough on the subject of eternal damnation for the wicked, a statement prompted by the recent inner-city riots and the escalating crime figures. Leaving aside the disastrous confusion between crime and serious sin, the implication that eternal damnation awaits the criminal classes alone, (did no one remind Robert Maxwell that the resurrection of the dead and the last judgement actually begin on the spot where he arranged for his body to be buried according to Jewish law?), and that the preaching of the gospel is basically a matter of social control, the real weakness of such statements is that they represent a grievous failure of communication between different cultures. In strict theology, the minister is right; a personal judgement awaits each of us. But, in Catholic Christian teaching, this truth is employed against the rich and powerful to 'pluck down the mighty from their seats', and never simply to confirm the successful and complacent in their pride of possession.

The problem is that the minister does accord ultimate value to the traditional *schema* of the Christian Church, whereas those whom he denounces (apparently) do not. If the prevailing culture is dominated by U & C Inc, then there is no after-life at all. Meaning and value are only to be found according to the laws of the corporation: I am what, or whom, I consume and what I have under my control. What does it matter if it is someone else's car that I take, or that I risk my life and that of others when I go joy riding? There is, after all, no ultimate significance to my life – or anyone else's. It is here, of course, that the joy riders and others are perhaps unconsciously calling the bluff of the Corporation: can you deliver to me the ultimate significance of my own life? Can you justify me? I will put it to the test, I will dance with you, I will dance with Death. There surely is the ultimate reality, the final curtain, that dominating final horizon from which you cannot redeem me! It is not for anyone to say of others what their motivation for doing this or that might be: such a judgement belongs to God alone. But that this is not an unreasonable interpretation of this particular form of criminal behaviour, and its incidental increase, can be argued from the writings and artistic offerings of the cultural establishment who for better or worse dominate the means of communication. And, in an excessively deferential society such as that of the United Kingdom, there will be powerful instruments and servants of the prevailing ethos. Together with the bankers, scientists and commentators, the artists are also dependent upon this culture of death, this conspiracy of silence in the face of ultimate reality, paid up members of U & C Inc, unless they declare to the contrary. 'He who is silent consents – ' is an old maxim of the law, and we must accept our own complicity in this silence!

Alienation from God

WHEN THE PAINTER Francis Bacon died, the media were full of nothing but praise for his achievements. To quote from them would be boring, what matters is that the establishment rallied round his interpretation of life, his meaning, and gave it their accolade and approval. What was this meaning, this vision of life which was accorded so prominent a place in the Pantheon of the contemporary world-view? Those familiar with Bacon's pictures will surely agree with the following comment by H. R. Rookmaaker in his *Modern Art and the Death of a Culture*:

Francis Bacon is a great English artist whose images are horrible to look at and haunt the imagination. Images of misery, of despair, of alienation, of decay, of a world in which paralytic, neurotic, leprous schizoids move in cages, human beings become animal and yet remain human, a world in which people are real even if lost in the void. Bacon's pictures are caricatures of mankind, not humorous images but great cries of despair for lost values and lost greatness, for a humanity deprived of its freedom, love, rationality.[2]

Bacon himself said about his art:

Also, man now realises that he is an accident, that he is a completely futile being, that he has to play out the game without reason. I think that when Velasquez or Rembrandt were painting, they were still slightly conditioned by certain types of religious possibilities, which man now has had cancelled out for him. Man now can only attempt to beguile himself for a time, by prolonging his life, by buying a kind of immortality through the doctors. You see painting has become – all art has become – a game by which man distracts himself.[3]

All that is left is that life should be made a bit more exciting. This is exactly what U & C Inc promises. In his study of suicide, *The Savage God*, A. Alvarez tries to describe:

that numbness – beyond hope, despair, terror and certainly beyond heroics – which is the final quantum to which all the modish forms of twentieth-century alienation are reduced. Under the energy, appetite and constant diversity of the modern arts is this obdurate core of blankness and insentience which no amount of creative optimism and effort can wholly break down or remove. It is like, for a believer, the final, unbudgeable illumination that God is not good.[4]

Elsewhere he suggests that the driving force behind the restless experimentalism of the twentieth-century arts is 'a sense of chaos' – the fear of meaninglessness:

More simply, just as the decay of religious authority in the nineteenth century made life seem absurd by depriving it of any ultimate coherence, so the growth of modern technology has made death itself absurd by reducing it to a random happening totally unconnected with the inner rhythms and logic of the lives destroyed.[5]

It would seem that despite man's need for a coherent system of values, our society seems to have abandoned the hope of finding one, beyond the most limited utility. The Warnock Report on *in vitro* fertilisation and embryology (1984) was honest enough to admit that its value system was 'the sort of society we praise and admire'.[6] Such subjectivity is perilously close to basing my sense of value on my own convenience or, more accurately, the convenience of the Corporation which wishes to add another area of human freedom to its holdings.

The Cosmic Christ

IF THIS ANALYSIS of our contemporary society and culture is basically correct, that we are haunted by a pervasive sense of meaninglessness or cosmic futility, then the clear duty of the Church is to reveal more clearly in proclamation and celebration precisely this dimension of her faith, as of first importance. The opening note to the liturgical celebration of Easter, at the Vigil on Saturday night, is one of cosmic significance. The words with which the celebrant cuts the cross into the paschal candle are concerned with the significance of the risen Christ for all time: yesterday and today, Alpha and Omega, beginning and end, all time belongs to him and all the ages. Human life, we now know, has come about after an immense length of time, and an immensely complicated period of development. We know that countless other species have come and gone, leaving only a fossil trace behind. But for their existence and extinction, sentient and self-conscious life could never have come about.

The resurrection of Christ – his bodily resurrection – is a vindication of this long 'agony' of creation, a vindication too of the primordial meaning and value which God gave to his handiwork 'in the beginning'. But for this event, even with belief in a good creator, I could never be certain that the distortion and corruption in the creation would not in the end overcome its goodness. As well as the redemption of history, the resurrection reveals the future for created reality. It is not doomed forever to decay and futility, but, passing away in its present form, it will pass over with Christ to that freedom from bondage of which St Paul speaks in Romans 8. It cannot be stressed too strongly that by bodily resurrection the Church means the very same body that was crucified and laid in the tomb. It *must* be this same body that was wounded and tortured that was raised to glory by the power of God. Anything less than this can offer at best a quasi-gnostic redemption through flight from time and materiality. Moreover, the dead body of Jesus is a kind of anti-sacrament of sin, the climax of human sin and rebellion against God, the judicial slaughter of the son of God. It is because the Church believes that Jesus' body was raised that she also believes in the forgiveness of sins. No longer does mankind have to carry that long history of sorrow engendered by his alienation from God.

'O happy fault', she sings in the *Exultet*. 'O necessary sin of Adam, that won for us so great a Saviour!' Restored to humanity in this event is our proper place within the meaning and order of the creation. Human persons are the image of God himself, his representatives or viceroys, set up in the temple of the cosmos. In Christ we have a vocation to rule with Christ's own kingly authority and after the pattern that he has given us and this, of course, is given at Pentecost when the handing over of the Spirit brings the paschal mystery to its completion.

The empowerment of the Spirit is the power to draw out from the creation that blessing with which God has endowed it, its inner moral order and meaning. As we do this, we are promised that we will experience the world ourselves as blessing. 'Seek ye first the kingly rule of God, and all these other things shall be added unto you'.[7]

There are two other aspects of the cosmic Christ that deserve our attention. The first concerns the ascension, or, as St John describes it, Christ's departure. At his ascension, Christ does not simply fade away. The glorification of his risen body means that it is co-extensive with all created reality. He is Lord of space as well as time. When we look up at the stars we should have the courage to say 'The Body of Christ'. This cosmic presence is the necessary precondition of his mystical and sacramental modes of presence in and for the Church.

It is only because he himself is the One who 'fills all things' that the Church can be his fullness, i.e. the effective sign of the unity of all mankind in God.[8] Here, the really critical celebration is the assumption of our Lady: she (model of the creation and of the Church) is portrayed as 'clothed with the sun, and with the moon under her feet and the with twelve stars about her head', because she is the first after Christ to experience resurrection reality. It is because Mary, who is pure creature, has put on the risen body of her Son in its fullness, that we the Church on earth may hope so to do also. The important thing is that it is *his* risen body with which she is clothed, his cosmic body.

The second coming

THE SECOND ASPECT of this mystery is Christ's return in glory together with the resurrection of the dead and the last judgement. What is at stake here is something absolutely crucial to the belief in moral order in creation. As will be known, until recently it appeared that our world was divided between two powerful and conflicting ideologies or systems. One has already been described in the course of this article: Unbelievers and Consumers Incorporated. The other is the socialist or communist Utopia. This latter system of belief and value promises to the people of the present that the perfect human society can be brought about in the future, and that those who have died before this perfectly just society can be established will somehow find their own justice when it comes about. The truth is that this has never and never can come about: what happens is that people who sacrifice themselves for a purely this-worldly future will have passed out of human history without receiving justice. This means that even were such a society to emerge, it could not do justice to the dead: rather the new society would have to live with the fact that the amount of injustice would always exceed the amount of justice in the world. This, of itself, would invalidate the claim of a perfect society and would give rise to that same ultimate fear of meaninglessness to human life.

The Church, on the other hand, believes in a kingdom which has already been inaugurated, and the pre-condition for enjoying its perfection is that we have begun to live according to its principles on earth: as Cardinal Ratzinger has trenchantly observed: 'Utopia is "no-where" and its time never comes.'[9] Perhaps the most crucial consideration here is how the Church celebrates death. The old custom of placing the paschal candle close to the coffin, acts as a reminder that *all* the Church's life and activity, including the last rites for the departed, flow out from her fundamental conviction concerning the resurrection of Christ and her ability to apply it in virtue of the Spirit. The Requiem Mass as prayer that the departed may have applied to them the full effects of Christ's resurrection is the norm for the Church and each believer. Memorial services or services in thanksgiving for the life of, however pastorally advisable, must not obscure the basic truth that only the resurrection of Christ can make sense of human death. However good or great the departed may have been in this life, or however unimportant in worldly terms, all alike await the same reality of judgement. 'Whatever the crime the same meal is served to all.'[10]

Nicholas Kavanagh is deputy vicar of Brighton.

Notes

1. 1 Corinthians 15.14–19
2. H. R. Rookmaaker *Modern Art and the Death of a Culture* (IVP, 1978) p. 173
3. *Ibid.* p. 174
4. A. Alvarez *The Savage God* (Penguin, 1974) p. 263
5. *Ibid.* p. 265
6. Ephesians 1.22–23
7. *Report of the Committee of Inquiry into Human Fertilisation and Embryology* (HMSO, 1984) p. 3
8. 'The Church, in Christ, is in the nature of sacrament – a sign and instrument that is – of communion with God and of unity among all men.' *Dogmatic Constitution on the Church, Lumen Gentium* (21 November, 1964)
9. *Considerations on the Instruction on Christian Freedom and Liberation, Communio* (1987)
10. Graham Greene *The Honorary Consul* (Penguin, 1980) p. 122

Intimate relationships, divine aspirations and human resources

Gillian Walton

'VICAR in sex row scandal.' This is well known by journalists to be a good selling main feature for a popular newspaper. Why should this be? Surely vicars are only human. Well, yes and no. It is deeply distressing to most communities if the conduct of the parish priest is other than exemplary – more so than if it were to be the doctor, lawyer or teacher, although they are not immune. The church authorities act congruently with this deep distress by regarding erring clergy as disgraced and by extending scant pastoral care to wives and families. Once the icon of the Holy Family is shattered, there is a heavy price to be paid. This is true also of the Royal Family and other public figures whose marriages, liaisons and family relationships are placed under microscopic scrutiny and often prurient interest which indicates a big investment in examining and judging the standards achieved.

How can we account for this great interest in committed human relationships as played out on the public screen of the church or those who lead public lives? This is a time when arguably there is a greater confusion of problems than hitherto in relationships: more liberalism, less dogmatism, more exploration of gender and a fear of the disintegration of the great 'given' of human society, heterosexual marriage. The statistics are well known. More than one in three marriages at present entered upon are predicted to end in divorce; there is a growing number of children brought up by one parent only and a complex problem of several partnerships and marriages giving rise to the so-called reconstituted family. Our multi-cultural society introduces still more varied patterns of marriage and family life and all this without the issues thrown up by the call from the homosexual community to have its relationships respected and indeed hallowed in the same way as heterosexual relationships.

How then can we account for the continued preoccupation with 'idealised' marriage and family life, given that many people consciously question if not overturn the ideal, and to which authority do Christians look for the legitimacy of their own relationships? Martin Richards, a Cambridge academic and researcher into contemporary marriage, makes the point that the more people experience failure and difficulty within their relationships the more they go after something ideal or perfect. One obvious source of inspiration and information to which Christians might turn is the Bible. In fact, rather few marriages are documented in any detail, and most of those that are, are very rich in conflict and far from ideal – Abraham and Sarah, Jacob and Rachel and Leah, David and Bathsheba. In the New Testament, marriage is regarded as secondary to mission, given the pressing urgency of the times and the imminent expectation of the 'second coming'. There was no question of our Lord's disciples staying at home with their wives and St Paul's fulfilment lay in the single life.

Nevertheless, similes of marriage abound in relation to Christ and the church and rules and conventions for the proper behaviour of men and women in relation to one another have guided the personal lives of Christians until very recently when the challenge from the women's movement and feminism has begun to be taken seriously. All this, arguably, has been a source of caricaturing and wounding to many men who have in turn felt extreme difficulty in convincing women that they are not violent, repressive potential rapists and the struggle within the Church over the role of women and in particular women's ordination mirrors a struggle that is also present in society.

What emerges then for men is a confused picture in which it is puzzling and perplexing to know where to place oneself – on the one hand to be identified as spinelessly liberal and standing for nothing, on the other hand to be caught up in some kind of repressive strength: the difference between a 'new man' or a Goliath figure.

Couples coming for therapy often find themselves caught in a dilemma. Women frequently complain that their partners take them for granted, and are 'not there' for them. They feel they have the more or less sole responsibility for what Susie Orbach, the feminist writer, calls the emotional labour in the relationship. They wish to be out in the world more: to be recognised as making a contribution which almost always means having a paid job, since work, as Freud said many years ago, is essential to the health of the human psyche and this is almost always signified by some financial reward. On the other hand, in order to do this a woman may have to give up a good deal in other areas, also necessary to her psychic and spiritual well-being – especially her role as mother. It often seems a no-win situation but in a society where value is measured so much in terms of work, status and money, it is difficult to hold out against the prevailing trend. Men in their turn have to adjust to accommodate this. Many men speak of their feeling of impotence in relation to the women's movement, while many others can see in it an opportunity to discover the more feminine side of themselves as they are more exposed to caring for very small children and experience their dependency, so often re-evoking wishes of their own to be allowed to be needy and dependent. Paradoxically, although women often claim that this is what they want from their partners, they also often find it difficult to accept since expression of feelings tends to be equated in men with wimpishness and spinelessness and the absence of masculinity – a no-win situation for men.

What emerges then, is a confused and confusing picture where some of the stereotype role models are fading to be replaced by we seem to know not what. We might speculate as to why this is happening and especially why now.

Underlying the troubles of modern couple relationships, one of the most important issues is disappointment. How do you manage if your fairy prince turns into a frog, or the lady at the ball into Cinderella? These are themes very well-known to the world of myth and fairy story, and nobody is immune to their power. We all have a very rich inner world and a need to find corresponding figures in the outside world on which to project our fantasies and images, so as to be able to test their reality. It is against this background that clergy marriage and family, as well as other public marriages, are projected and judged. In them are invested a good deal of unmet expectation, but they are also a source of considerable envy, and that makes them extra vulnerable. It is very difficult when our own hopes are frustrated or disappointed to allow others to have the life we would ideally have wanted for ourselves. The attitude to the Royal Family is a good example of this ambivalence. There is a need for them to be ideal and have ideal marriages, yet the prurient interest in them and the wish to find all their weaknesses makes even a fairly normal life impossible, and they find themselves vulnerable to the same difficulty to stay married as anyone else.

Some of the evidence for the changes in patterns of marriage and other close relationships comes from the research and writing of contemporary sociologists, and in the changes in legislation. The relaxation of the divorce laws in England and Wales in 1969, and in Scotland in 1976 led to an increase in the number of people seeking a legal ending to their marriages. There is nevertheless the debate as to whether the more liberal divorce laws are a cause or an effect of marriage break-down. Interestingly, the most common time for divorce to occur is around the eighth year of marriage so that the majority involve young children, 90 per cent of whom live with their mothers. Many people re-marry. The current estimate is that one marriage in three is a re-marriage for one of the partners, so that what is now called the 're-constituted' family is a reality for many children, some of whom may even more or less live in two families. Moreover, because of increased longevity, we now have the reality of marriages surviving into old age. This is very much a latter day phenomenon, and the reality as opposed to the fantasy of older married people is a component of the scene surrounding contemporary marriage. It would be impossible to write of present day couples without mention of homosexual relationships. While studies of homosexual activity suggest that up to one-third of adult men and women have at some time been engaged in sexual activity with someone of the same sex, those who commit themselves to a more permanent or public relationship are a smaller, but nevertheless more recognised group in the 1980s and '90s. However, these relationships and heterosexual relationships generally have been greatly influenced by HIV and AIDS. The very real risk and fear of contracting the disease has enormous potential, both clinical and psychological, for threatening and confronting marriages and all couple relationships. It is forcing to the surface issues of monogamy, trust, fidelity and renegotiation of relationships, especially in view of the fact that studies show that possibly as many as 73 per cent of people in first or second marriages may have had affairs.

How much social changes are driven by the inner changes or vice-

versa is a conundrum, but the growing focus on the importance of
the human psyche and the growth of respect for each individual as
having some right to achieve his or her personal potential is an
ebbing and flowing theme throughout human history, and certainly
in the history of Britain. Often these movements for human rights
have been cloaked in religious struggles – the Lollards, the Puritan
movement in the sixteenth century which coincided with and drove
the movement for more parliamentary participation, and the Metho-
dists in the eighteenth century would be examples of this, as would
the Evangelical and the Village Evangelist movements later. In all
these groups, an attempt was made to move the power base from
an exclusive group and to recognise the value and potential of a much
wider group so that their gifts and capacities could be recognised and
used. In the nineteenth century important developments began to
take place, in the biological and human sciences. Significant amongst
these, was the work of Charles Darwin whose *Origin of Species*
rocked the established world as Galileo and Copernicus had done
earlier, and at the same time there was growing interest in the human
psyche as a focus for study. This was, of course, taken furthest by
Freud whose early work on human sexuality deeply shocked his
contemporaries. Perhaps what is highlighted by the response to these
new ideas is how terrifying it is for most people to contemplate
change, especially when first introduced. It gives rise to the very
human and normal reaction of retrenchment and flight, but sometimes this has damaging and crippling effects on oneself and others.
A reading of Edmund Gosse's *Father and Son*, a story of a brilliant
natural scientist, a contemporary of Darwin, whose own life and that
of his son was crippled by his inability to dare to think any new
thoughts is a salutary tale, and all in the name of Christianity. Jung
reflected in his autobiography *Memories, Dreams and Reflections*
about the grace that is released by following the true promptings of
God, rather than remaining hide-bound by dogma as he perceived
in his father and the senior Reformed churchmen of his close
acquaintance, even if those promptings seemed at the time to lead
into dangerous areas:

'So that was it!' I felt an enormous, an indescribable relief. Instead
of the expected damnation, grace had come upon me and with it an
unutterable bliss such as I had never known . . . A great many things

I had not previously understood became clear to me. That was what my father had not understood, I thought he had failed to experience the will of God, had opposed it for the best reasons and out of deepest faith and that was why he had never experienced the miracle of grace which heals all and makes all comprehensible.'[1]

The fundamental belief of those who work in the field of the human psyche is that many of us are not in a good relationship with ourselves, and that by refusing to acknowledge whole areas, we are depriving ourselves of the ability to be fully alive. Jesus said: 'Whosoever will save his life will lose it; and whosoever will lose his life for my sake shall find it.'[2] Certainly in letting go comes great peace, healing and reconciliation, but is there not a danger in it as well? In our own generation, perhaps the most recent mass experience of a 'letting go' was in the 1960s when it appeared to go right across the board. It was a coincidence of the results of questioning and soul-searching in a number of areas. For example, the issue of the relationship between love, sex and marriage was increasingly debated in public, and was raised explicitly in the 1962 Reith Lectures given by G. M. Carstairs. He questioned whether chastity was the supreme moral virtue, and suggested that mutual consideration and more fundamental satisfaction might be more important ingredients of a good marriage. Some churchmen in the early 1960s were also taking publicly a more radical view, amongst them the Bishop of Woolwich who apparently rejected traditional thinking on marriage and divorce and argued that the significant factor in all relationships was their basis in love, without which nothing had meaning. It led to the position being taken that pre-marital sex, extra-marital sex or divorce could not be labelled as wrong unless it lacked love. In 1963 came the publication of *Towards a Quaker View of Sex* which again emphasised that sexual morality came from within, condemned the emphasis on morality which often was accompanied by a 'cold and inhibitive attitude' and argued that the hallmark of wrong behaviour was the exploitation of another human being, and that society as a whole would benefit from the love, warmth and generosity which would be released as a result of this paradigm shift.[3]

The writings of Martin Buber, the Jewish philosopher, who stressed the ontological significance of the encounter between the I and Thou, and his famous phrase, 'all life is meeting', influenced many of these writers and thinkers, as did the influx of, often highly adapted, eastern religious thought. The 1960s explosion of youth culture, the contraceptive pill and sexual experimentation, mood-altering drugs, and a general questioning of inherited values was a heady mixture and the continued reverence for some of its prime movers is a testament to its perceived significance.

What of the present and the future? Perhaps a lasting aftermath has been the recognition of each individual's need to search for meaning for himself or herself, and that this search can follow a number of different pathways. One of the problems, though, is that the commitment to a belief in the importance of each person to pursue his own happiness and fulfillment has a potentially disintegrating effect on the concept of community. This applies also to marriage, commitment and family. Mrs Thatcher's famous statement, 'There is no such thing as society', stressing instead the position of the individual is indicative of this. An illustration from marital therapy might be a husband who cannot understand why his wife is desperately hurt by his having re-discovered a sense of self-worth after a brief affair.

Perhaps one of the most damaging effects of individualism in terms of couple relationships is the pain and distress caused to children by the loss of a parent through separation or divorce, since inevitably they take on some of the guilt and responsibility for not having been 'good enough' to keep the parent from leaving. However, is it really preferable to live in a state of slavish adherence to a spiritually, or emotionally meaningless or possibly physically damaging moral imperative? The multiplicity of different experiences of 'family' in contemporary Britain means that to predicate a standard model is increasingly difficult, so what is the basis for the future expectations of the present generation of children and young people?

The need to have an intimate, committed couple relationship is fundamental to human nature. Time and time again, couples with appalling experiences of broken homes come for help in order to repair and redeem in their own adult lives some of the damaging experiences of childhood. The more their own models are experienced as wanting, the more difficult it is to achieve something different. Marriage is an archetype, the end of all fairy stories. It provides an opportunity to rediscover the intimacy and exclusiveness of a child with a loving parent. Being committed to another human being, especially early in the relationship, affords a sense of unity and harmony, a return to what Jung described as 'that original condition of unconscious oneness . . . that is like a return to childhood.'[4] It is when this unconscious state no longer holds, in the period 'after the honeymoon' that there is a danger. It is at this point when disappointment may come in and when the need for the marriage to hold firm as a container while the process of individuation begins is most urgent. This is in any case a difficult process, but perhaps especially difficult in a culture geared to results, instant emotion and intense individualism, and where marriage as an institution is relatively poorly supported by the state. It might be said that there are so many different experiences of close couple relationships that it is meaningless to talk of a standard couple or a standard family. Nevertheless, evidence from the world of marital therapy would suggest that people do struggle very hard to achieve the intimacy with one other human being that they long for and that it causes great distress when the relationship ends. The aspirations are present to achieve intimacy and love, and to achieve this within a nurturing and containing relationship. There has been a revolt against hypocrisy and cant, but there is danger that in the vacuum that has been left by the overthrow of some of the old imperatives comes alienation, and a search for meaning which is inadequately met, sometimes filled by a rigid fundamentalism, so great is people's need for security.

It is perhaps in view of this difficulty that such pressure is put on public marriages to show the way. The clergy who at their ordinations have to promise to 'order their households' have a most awesome task to live out for others, as do the Royal Family whose marriages are 'attended' by audiences of millions and on to whom are projected the hopes and expectations of many people engaged in a similar struggle. If the icons fail what hope for the rest? But these icons are also vulnerable to have projected on to them the blame and failure felt by the onlookers in their own lives, and are often judged harshly.

Where does all this leave the Church, and what are the implications for Christians trying to make sense of the changing patterns? There is a danger of its becoming preoccupied by the debate whether to re-marry divorced people in church rather than by how to support those who are experiencing difficulties and needing support. It is often anxiety that leads to a wish to make rules and form judgements but it is nurture and support that is needed. Again, to quote Jung:

One should take great care not to interrupt this necessary development by acts of moral violence, for any attempt to create a spiritual attitude by splitting off and suppressing the instincts is a falsification. Nothing is more repulsive than a furtively prurient spirituality.[5]

In 1978, a General Synod Report *Marriage and the Church's Task*, talking of the expectations placed on marriage, stated:

If marriage has to fulfil these high expectations, the emphasis on the relationship between husband and wife no longer butressed by clear-cut social roles, strong extended family networks and economic pressures which often made the splitting up of the marriage home unthinkable, demands a great deal of them.[6]

Clearly, extending love and support to those who struggle to find meaning within their relationships and who attempt not to hurt or be hurt is fundamental.

This was, of course, the way of Jesus who took men and women where they were and as they were and accepted their nature until they reached the point at which they were able to turn and repent and accept him, but all was based on love and the relationship of person to person, and the person with his or her own inner life. This is costly work since it involves a constant dialogue within oneself within the context of the life of prayer and of the sacraments to discern what is truly the way of Love and therefore of God. This does not mean a life of *laisser faire*. Sometimes it is more loving to confront issues and encounter conflict, as Jesus did not flinch from doing, than to take the line of blind acceptance.

The Church is wrestling in public with issues on behalf of society, such as fidelity, commitment, sexuality, the role of men and women, managing public and private life, and the suitable upbringing of children. These are issues which concern and trouble everyone and the pain they cause within the Church is a mirror of their universal importance. There are implications for the selection, training and support of clergy, but they are issues in which all Christians are involved and which go right to the heart of the gospel which is about Good News and New Life.

Gillian Walton is a marital psychotherapist and head of training and supervision at the London Marriage Guidance.

Notes

1. C. G. Jung *Memories, Dreams and Reflections* (Fontana, 1983) p. 56
2. Matthew 16.25
3. Ed. Alastair Heron *Towards a Quaker View of Sex* (Friends Home Service Committee, 1963)
4. C. G. Jung *The Development of Personality*: Collected Works vol. 17 (Routledge, 1991) p. 192
5. *Ibid.* p. 197
6. *Marriage and the Church's Task* (Church Information Office Publishing, Church House, 1978)

Pride and Prejudices

Sister Agatha Mary

'PRIDE AND PREJUDICES. Of course, we all have them,' we say, 'they're natural.' And although that naturalness makes them neutral as far as our moral balance-sheet is concerned, we are left with some questions that continue to flash in and out of our minds, posing one set of problems and then another.

Where does it all begin, this instinctively negative attitude that we all have towards certain experiences that come our way? Why do we shrink from this encounter, that idea or the other event? What do we really mean when we talk about our proper pride? How do we handle our many prejudices? When will we be able to reach the end of the flashing questions?

Our pride and our prejudices are pretty harmless, we think. But are they? Pride is centred on my self and all that I identify with. Prejudice is centred on my concerns, tastes and needs. Pride and prejudice may not hurt us, or at any rate we do not always feel the hurt; but, more often than we realise, they do hurt other people. Most likely, we only recognise or admit that fact when we ourselves are the victim. It takes us a very long time to learn that we are not the only persons in our world, that there are others who are saying the words that we say: 'I am myself, I know what I like and I know what I want.' The importance of *me* is either the biggest lie or the biggest truth within each one of us, and allowing the truth to overcome the lie is the work of a lifetime.

When we ourselves are the victim of another's prejudice, most often it is the biggest lie in me that causes me to suffer: I cannot accommodate within myself the 'I' of another that is so different from me. I cannot make room for the other. I feel threatened by the demands of that other.

Outside my window where I sit writing there is a tiny hole in the wall which for many years has been a battle-ground when nesting time begins and sparrows, tits and starlings all claim rights of entry for the season. Sometimes one species stakes the first claim, but it may well happen that after several days of bickering and a few open fights one of the contenders takes over and raises a family there, while the other two with disgruntled twitterings have to look elsewhere for somewhere to call their own. I think, too, of the one fledgling cuckoo that has the misfortune to be laid and hatched in a chaffinch's nest; its need for food and space is so much larger than theirs. From the cuckoo's point of view it is not doing a shocking thing when it throws some of its companions out of their home so that it can thrive. Wherever there is life there is a threat against life. For human beings, it is the response to the experience of threat that lies at the heart of all our prejudices, for prejudice is what we develop in order to exclude the effects of whatever threatens us.

Similarly with our pride, our unbalanced self-esteem: we are in constant dread of having it hurt, and our mechanisms of self-defence span the whole spectrum of human ingenuity. Pride has its roots in our self-awareness and the value that we set on our self. Whether our self-estimation is, in fact, negative or positive the same thing is true. Paradoxically, it is the person who has a very poor self-opinion who has the greatest dread of being hurt by others. Pride is our reaction to whatever presents itself as a threat; and what is potentially threatening is anything that lies beyond our control because we cannot identify with it experientially. We can be proud of being black, but if all people were black there would be no cause for being proud. When we were children we were proud of our school, but if there had been only one school anywhere there would have been no cause for pride in belonging to it (although we would very likely have distinguished ourselves from the children who had no schooling at all). As adults, we might be proud of a pacifist position, but if all were of this mind the very term would not exist.

I could continue making this list until bedtime, but I must stop writing now because in a minute or two I have to be at choir practice. 'Choir practice?' Yes, choir practice. 'Put on your outdoor things, grab your music and go scurrying to some church or hall?' No, because the practice takes place in the building where I live and where all the other singers live too. The writing of these reflections of mine has to be dovetailed into quite a large number of other activities that go to make up my day; and I have mentioned this here because I have been asked to write on the subject of pride and prejudice from my point of view as one who belongs to a religious community whose members are in constant contact with each other all day and every day with only occasional changes of scenery.

Life's experience has given to me and to all sisters a load of pride and prejudices: not that we think of the matter in those terms when we enter the convent. We come, just as we are, with our mixture of high ideals and low weaknesses which, if we *are* aware of them, we hope no one else will notice. But it is not long before everyone else in the group begins to put pride and prejudice labels on us. And, if we are still holding to our ideals and our awareness of being called to this sort of life, then we begin to admit to ourselves that those labels do describe what is in us. Our previous life-experience may already have given us reason to judge that the P & P label can be put on some of our sisters, but unless we are prepared to accept such a label personally we are never going to grow up. Shrinking from criticism is one of the many infantilisms that persist. So many of our preconceptions have to go; until they have done so, we are bound to be jarring on other members of the community.

At this point the words pride and prejudice have to be abandoned, I think. For once a would-be sister comes off the pink cloud where she put herself after she had been accepted as an aspirant to the religious life (and come off it she certainly must), such polished words are only a mask covering the negative aspect of the experience of living and working with a disparate group of people. Only one word is unvarnished enough to be real in a situation like ours, and that is *intolerance*.

In some form or other, every one of us experiences a large measure of intolerance and we spend our lives learning to deal with it. Some of us cannot tolerate incompetence, or what we judge to be bad manners, or what is indubitably a voice singing flat, or a person who cannot stand still in chapel, or one who has a loud laugh. Many feel threatened by a witty tongue that can sound malicious, or by a sharp mind that can see a faulty argument a mile off, or by an habitual tone of voice, or by the introduction of changes that affect something we love dearly. Others are inhibited by the abilities or skills or personal charm of others. All of us, at some time or other, feel threatened by the very demands that our way of life makes on us:

the necessity of stopping a piece of writing because it is time for choir practice, the fact that we may not find the person we need to consult because she is praying, the fact that willy-nilly we have to live with a collection of people who can occasionally (we think) reach the very frontiers of tiresomeness.

In the common experience that I have described in the previous paragraph and which, I think, reflects that of human beings in whatever *milieu* they spend their lives, it is possible to see that all the way through we are both victims and perpetrators of a real hostility that arises from intolerance. Making room for difference is the difficult task that it is simply because of our finitude – both time and space are limited. In one sense, we always feel the squeeze. In fact, travelling by public transport in the rush hour is a mirror image of what life is like both inside and outside monasteries and convents. Perhaps what happens daily in trains and buses is an example of the art of living. Yes, we do fear being crushed, not being able to reach the exit when we want to get out, having our pocket picked or our body knifed; but we accept all of this with a pretty high degree of equanimity, recognising that we are all suffering in the same way.

* * *

THE REALISATION of a common identity and an awareness that we are the cause of suffering to others are the ingredients that begin to dissolve intolerance. This dissolving cannot happen until we acknowledge what we are doing to other people. We have to learn to speak in love. We need also to let our needs and our foibles, as well as our hurts, be known. All of that is a painful process, but until we have reached the point of being willing to be hurt we shall never overcome the intolerance that is in us.

Being hurt is itself a challenge because it can trigger off anger, in which case the experience of hurt is a wasted opportunity. It seems that in this sort of situation we are angry because of our dread of another's power – the fact that someone has the power to disturb our self-made equilibrium. The hurt is something that we have to accept, it is something that is actually happening to us. We shall not lose that pain until we move out from our wounded self towards the person who has hurt us – until, that is, we have accepted the hurter as well as the hurt. And this is the very thing that we are frightened of doing. So the estrangement increases; it grows on and on indefinitely if we do nothing to stop it. What happens then is that each is exercising great power to injure the other.

Most of us, I rather think, must plead guilty on this score if we are honest. Many things displease us, which is an entirely reasonable state of affairs since we are not all alike. We find some things thoroughly intolerable – and sometimes it is entirely right that we should find them so, for since we have knowledge of good and evil we cannot avoid finding some things completely unacceptable. But, as persons, we are demeaned by the deplorable ways in which we so often act out our varying degrees of intolerance. Therefore, the first thing necessary if we want to keep intolerance under control, is to be thoroughly honest.

Honesty, then, compels us to admit that we possess a number of intolerable characteristics in our make-up. The result is an ugly picture. I begin with the assumption that intolerance is embedded in us. Allowing this component in our personhood to have free play will certainly warp our judgement. It will make us very unrealistic in our attitude towards, and our expectations of, the people and situations that we find unacceptable. We are bound to undervalue them and to miscalculate their capacity for good. And, although we shall, as a consequence, often act impetuously towards them we shall at the same time be hidebound with regard to the criteria that we use for forming our judgment. Even though those we are oppressing may show estimable qualities that lie outside the range of our intolerance we are not likely to change our attitude; instead we shall become very jealous and will easily become downright malicious in our behaviour. For what we are doing with our antipathy is using it to threaten, harass and dominate others.

* * *

SO FAR I have explored intolerance in terms of the prides and prejudices that we display in our ordinary social experience. Now we must look at what happens in the global context of our lives. As I have said, our difficulty is that we cannot identify with what we cannot understand, and there are so many phenomena that do lie beyond our experience. Most of us belong to a particular country, and people from other countries are outsiders to us. We respond to our own culture but are highly suspicious of many differing ones. We are fully aware of the colour of our pigmentation and we have no idea what it is like to live inside a skin of another colour. Even if colour does not disturb, many people are suspicious of the religious beliefs and practices of others; to a large extent we are all outsiders to most of the world's religions and because we do not understand them we are likely to regard them as mysterious (forgetting that each one is concerned to approach the mystery that is God himself). Our lack of understanding and our experience of being an outsider is an important factor also in the deep antagonisms of sexism in all its forms.

In these large areas, where so many people are both victims and perpetrators of intolerance we have to look very carefully at both aspects of our problem. The sensation of threat and of being unable to cope with otherness is even sharper here than it is in our ordinary everyday aversions, and we go to greater extremes to protect our own self-interest. We form movements, we protest, demonstrate, write letters to MPs and to the press: all of this is an attempt to strengthen our fortifications against invasion by something that is alien to ourselves. Yet, throughout history growth and development have come about through accepting and understanding the invader. Today, when communication is widespread and quick, battle-lines and war-cries seem to be increasing, and a lot of time and energy is spent in finding out who is for us and who is against. Somewhere along the line there are those who are for us and those who are against, and we feel safe if we can be sure of what others think: hence the emergence of the poll-taking industry. We make allies and we make enemies, overlooking the fact that at heart what everyone wants is to live in peace.

* * *

HOW, THEN, can we survive, when we are surrounded by so many factors that we find wholly unassimilable?

In spite of all our differences, however deep they may be, we all want to live in peace and unity; and what we are looking for now are ways that point in the right direction although they do not take us immediately to our goal.

The first necessity is not to turn one's back on the things that we do not like nor to pretend that they do not exist. In an ordinary setting there are times when we are wise to distance ourselves from an area of conflict that is too complicated for us to handle; but for the most part we have to dare to stand still and listen to what is happening. Our very awareness of an ill, whether it be global or domestic, lays on us a duty to explore its implications in order to find the way to healing. Each of us who pretends that nothing is really wrong, or who merely hopes for the best that things will get sorted out if left alone, is living in a fool's paradise. Ignorance is a very fruitful soil for intolerance to grow in.

The second necessity is a willingness to have one's own attitude changed in some respects, because unless we can be open and objective we shall never be able to see what lies behind the thinking and behaviour that we find unacceptable: what is apartheid about, or feminism, or terrorism? Hiding behind our own prejudices and fears, however justified they may seem to be, is a destructive way of living.

And so a further way of dealing with otherness is a willingness to take risks. Every peace-maker does this, as we see very well in terms of both international affairs and of family quarrels. Peace and understanding are costly things to achieve, and we sometimes rue the day that we ever began tackling a difficulty; but to withdraw with the task half done will in most cases only make matters worse.

From this I think it follows that we have to be humble enough to recognise our own weaknesses, for everything that stirs resentment or abhorrence in us is a symbol of what is hidden in our own darkness. When we can accept our own vulnerability we are better able to discern the vulnerability of those with whom we disagree.

At this point we have to be on our guard against condescension. Crude pity for those whose weaknesses we see is not an attitude that will strengthen and change them; only compassion will do that. 'My brother is my life,' the Staretz Silouan said.[1] It is a rather daunting truth that our lives are reflected in the lives of those around us – for good or for ill. You only need one person in a thoroughly bad mood to infect a whole group of people in next to no time. Unless the mood can be accepted immediately with compassion and deflected from its destructive course there will be a major battle before anyone has time to get out of the room.

So, for some people, the building up of a personal store of patience is a high priority, and this is something that we are not going to develop very well unless we begin the process on the right side of forty. By the time we are heading for our half century, if our earlier exuberance and zeal have not been tempered by patience we are likely to become highly intolerant as we get older because our defensive mixture of prejudices and antagonisms will increase with our years. Patience, on the other hand, is the gate leading to a very fertile field.

For patience is the point of entry into an ongoing experience of understanding, companionship, shared tasks, shared ideas. Once more, I could extend this catalogue much further, but that is not necessary. With the help of patience we move out of the area of conflict into which our pride and prejudice lead us, and we come to see otherness as the creative thing that it really is. We move, that is, into a way of living that is exhilarating and often sheer fun.

* * *

ALL THAT I have written above is concerned with the anatomy of intolerance, like a doctor describing a disease. But no disease represents the wholeness of the person who is ill: there is so much more to us than our illness. We endure intolerance, whether actively or passively, in a life-situation that has many other components as well. In Northern Ireland, South Africa, East Timor and in many other stricken places people are receiving and giving goodness in ways that do not hit the headlines even while their suffering is being recorded in notebooks and on film. Whatever our circumstances we experience much that does not distress or harm us; we are in touch with so much that is good and lovely. Many people and events bring us great enjoyment. All these positive elements in our lives are a vital factor if we are to overcome the sombre weaknesses that most of this essay has been describing.

The ugly side of our interior and exterior lives is as real as the beautiful side, and it will not escape us as long as we live. We do all fall back and follow the leads that our pride and our prejudices provide for us; we all continue to inflict wounds on one another. When we were children we were taught to say 'I'm sorry' when that was appropriate. At the end of our lives, please God, we shall still be saying it when it is necessary. Just those words, sincerely meant, are a wonderful solvent. They are what the participants in a family row at the kitchen sink, as well as those seated round a formal table at international peace talks, are wanting to hear and must be ready to utter.

When John Donne wrote *A Hymne to God the Father* he had his own intolerable weaknesses in mind, but his words can be said by everyone who knows what intolerance itself is like.

> Wilt thou forgive those sinnes, through which I runne,
>   And do run still: though still I do deplore?
>   When thou hast done, thou hast not done,
>   For I have more.
>
> Wilt thou forgive that sinne by which I've wonne
>   Others to sinne? and, made my sinne their doore?
> Wilt thou forgive that sinne which I did shunne
>   A yeare, or two: but wallowed in, a score?
>   When thou hast done, thou hast not done,
>   For I have more.
>
> I have a sinne of feare, that when I have spunne
>   My last thred, I shall perish on the shore;
> Sweare by thy self, that at my death thy sonne
>   Shall shine as he shines now, and heretofore;
>   And, having done that, Thou hast done,
>   I feare no more.[2]

Thank God, we are all held in his mercy.

Sister Agatha Mary is a member of the Society of the Precious Blood, an Anglican contemplative community whose Mother House is at Burnham Abbey, Buckinghamshire. She is the author of The Rule of Saint Augustine: An Essay in Understanding.

Notes

1. Archimandrite Sofrony *The Undistorted Image* (Faith Press, 1956) p. 123.
2. *Complete Poetry and Selected Prose* (Nonesuch Press, 1932) p. 321.

Living with violence

Martin Israel

'BLESSED are the peacemakers: they shall be called God's children.'
So runs the familiar beatitude of Matthew 5.9. Jesus is familiarly
called the Prince of Peace, yet he comes not to bring peace, but a
sword. He has come to set members of families against each other,
so that a man will find enemies under his own roof (Matthew
10.34–36). The gospel is not unacquainted with paradox, but this
one is surely the most glaring. And yet the earlier prophets of Israel
were constantly railing against the false prophets who foretold peace
when there was no peace. The most dramatic episode occurs in the
twenty-eighth chapter of the Book of Jeremiah, where there is an
open conflict between Jeremiah and the false prophet Hananiah,
who predicted an early return home of the Israelite exiles from
Babylon with implicit peace once more in Judah. Jeremiah was
doubtful; 'The prophets who preceded you and me from earliest
times have foretold war, famine and pestilence for many lands and
for great kingdoms. If a prophet foretells prosperity, it will be known
that the Lord has sent him only when his words come true' (Jeremiah
28.8–9). Of course, Hananiah's prophecy is false, and he himself
soon dies as a punishment for misleading the nation in the name of
God.

Why does Jeremiah take such a gloomy view of authentic prophecy? Because he knows that the nation is sinful, and that until it
repents absolutely of its past and vows positively to change its mind
in the future, only hardship can continue. This is the law of cause
and effect, enunciated well by St Paul in Galatians 6.7–8. God is not
fooled; everyone reaps what he sows. This state of affairs is not to
be seen as the personal punishment meted out by a vengeful God,
but merely an application of the fundamental laws whereby life and
society are governed. If one transgresses a law, its penalties come
down clearly on the person even if some time may have to elapse
before a baneful effect is visible in that individual's life. On an

individual level there may be a deterioration of health (smoking and cancer, alcohol and cirrhosis of the liver, sexual promiscuity and venereal disease are three clear examples), while communal disobedience leads to frayed relationships that find their end in conflict. On a wider level this may boil over into sectarian or even national violence. And yet we have seen that Jesus comes to bring just that circumstance into human lives.

Violence seems to be near the core of competitive existence. We see it in animal existence where one species feeds on another: 'Nature red in tooth and claw', reflects Tennyson sadly in *In Memoriam*. In fact, animals are more merciful to each other than are humans; they take what they need for survival but do not store food in a gluttonous way. It seems a libel to the animal creation when an especially odious human act is described as bestial. The superior human mentality, while being capable of enormous feats in the realms of art and science when fully open to the creative power of the universe which we call God the Holy Spirit in Christian theology, can descend to infernal depths when completely centred in itself. It could well be that in such a situation it is dangerously open to infestation by demonic forces issuing from psychic depths beyond our normal understanding. When the early representatives of the human species hunted and gathered for food they may have produced no great civilisations, but neither did they produce the havoc on the environment and destruction of nature which is such a feature of the insensitive, often brutalised humans of our own century. As the human developed so did the capacity to think and differ.

There are three degrees of diversity of opinion: disagreement, conflict and violence. The first is mental and civilised, the second emotional and threatening, and the last physical and destructive. I believe we all have a focus of violence within our psyche, intent on preserving our own interests at all costs. If words do not suffice we threaten with action. It all points to the lack of security that seems an integral part of our life in this world. Those who are psychologically disturbed will resort to violence at the slightest provocation; they form the bulk of our prison population, and among them are members who actually exult in the destruction they produce. These 'psychopathic' people are also found among political and religious demonstrators. The sectarian murders in Northern Ireland have a psychopathic ring to them, plausibly attributed as they are to religious issues. Probably more violence and cruelty have been committed in the name of religion than for any other cause. Religion has in fact been the excuse for the liberation of violent impulses in people full of hatred against society as a whole, especially if we include the ghastly twentieth-century heresies of fascism and communism amongst the religious fraternity. A religion in this sense can be defined as a way of life that claims to lead people to the complete actualisation of their potentialities so that they can live a fully satisfying existence.

A notable feature of any aberrant religious system – and this may include the fully recognised religions also when they are in the hands of fanatics – is blind hatred of a particular class, race or occupational group that are alleged to pollute the sacred blood stream of society. Hatred seems to be an essential part of violence committed by relatively normal people. It could be argued that no normal person would act violently except under extreme provocation, in which case a practical definition of mental 'normality' would be a state of mind in which the individual could carry out the usual functions of everyday life so uneventfully as to arouse no comment from those in the vicinity. Such an individual could not claim to be healthy in mind, showing the difference between normality and health. It is little wonder that Christ came not to heal the healthy but the sick, not to call the virtuous but sinners (Mark 2.17). The irony of the situation was that those who thought they were healthy were in most need of healing; the normal were the most distressed. Likewise it was those who believed themselves righteous that precipitated Jesus's execution, whereas the rank and file merely followed on mindlessly: on one day they hailed his entry into Jerusalem and shortly afterwards they joined the communal cry to crucify him. Indeed, they needed forgiveness, for they did not know what they were doing at the instigation of others (Luke 19.35–38 followed by Luke 23.20–23 and 34).

People dedicated to thoroughly laudable issues can explode into dangerous violence against those whom they believe are obstructing the cause of virtue and decency. Thus 'animal rights' enthusiasts are notorious for their destructive zeal against research institutes that use animals as part of their experimental apparatus, often not using sufficient discrimination to judge what is of real value to human and animal health so that wanton destruction may put back the treatment of presently incurable diseases. On the other hand, it must be acknowledged that some animal research in the past was done primarily to afford publications by ambitious young workers looking for promotion in their particular specialities. It is doubtful, though, whether the violent tactics of some enthusiasts has deterred this questionable practice as much as better informed propaganda used to enlighten the general public about the abuse of animals for personal gain. The ecological crisis of the present time has added its quota of warning about the importance of all life in the sustenance of our planet.

In the same way people dedicated to the cause of pacifism have on occasions acted belligerently to those in charge of military installations, especially in connection with nuclear energy. Such behaviour, apart from necessitating the deployment of considerable numbers of police in the area, has done little to minimize the danger of nuclear attack or destruction. What makes people behave in this violent way even when espousing noble causes, and indeed what makes them espouse such causes in the first case? This general question can be extended to religious devotion also, except that spiritual matters are less immediately tangible than are those regarding animal rights and world peace. Thomas Babington Macaulay made this controversial observation in his *History of England*; 'The Puritan hated bear-bating, not because it gave pain to the bear, but because it gave pleasure to the spectators.' Although, no doubt, a little unfair, there is sufficient truth in this diagnosis of the human condition to make us think. It is often, although not always, the unhappy, unfulfilled type of individual who sets about putting the world to rights; his or her endeavour serves to take the mind off a personal problem and on to a general public cause, sometimes indeed being a focus on which the inadequacy can be projected. One thinks of Jesus' far from jocular injunction to get the beam out of our own eye before we start helping others to see properly (Matthew 7.3–5).

In the Parable of the Publican and the Pharisee (Luke 18.9–14) it is the wretched tax-collector who leaves the temple at rights with God, having been acquitted of his sins after his heart-felt confession and request for forgiveness. By contrast, the self-satisfied pharisee is so full of his piety that he is unaware of his sinful nature, made evident in his arrogant and unloving dismissal of his fellow worshipper, the tax-gatherer. If one can extend the parable in one's imagination – a very useful exercise in relation to many of the stories in both the Old and the New Testaments – one could imagine a future hardship befalling both men, say a period of economic stress associated with a recession such as we are currently experiencing. The pious one would be very angry that his religion had yielded so few tangible dividends, his wrath might be visited on aliens who seemed to be doing better than he, whom he might accuse of being parasitic infidels, and soon his displeasure might boil over into violence, made worse by his fellow worshippers experiencing similar emotional turmoil. The story of the rise of Hitler to power in a financially distraught Germany in the thirties is too close a reminder of such a sequence of events to leave us feeling comfortable. The forgiven tax-gatherer, on the other hand, would be so full of God's grace that he would feel little anger but would instead exert himself to assist all who were in need, in so doing actually discharging the residual debt that his past career had accumulated.

The road to hell is paved with too many good intentions, brought into practice by emotionally disturbed people. The narrow path that leads to heaven that Jesus speaks of in Matthew 7.14 may contain only a few travellers, but one may be sure that many of these are converted sinners who have found the love of God the only reality in life. It would be as impossible for them to ill-treat an animal as to hurt a criminal, as impossible to charge for their services as to judge those whose fees were exorbitant. Instead, they would be ever mindful of their early behaviour, thanking God that they were saved from its consequence in time, and devoting the remainder of their life to spreading the love of God abroad to all they met and prayed over. This is the way of love, but its full impress comes late in the lives of even sincere believers. It is the ego that gets in the way, whether a personal, collective or national ego. It demands, like the early-working labourers in the vineyard, just recompense – or what it feels is just – and is infuriated when others, apparently less worthy than itself, gets a similar reward (Matthew 20.1–16). That it should rejoice that other people have also gained the reward and the happiness coming from it, is quite inconceivable. Justice is embraced in this attitude, but there is no love; that the late-comers had been deprived of the personal satisfaction of a full day's work which they themselves had enjoyed simply does not penetrate their minds. Perhaps later on, when they too were out of work because of general unemployment or personal ill-health, they might be able to see the larger issues of the case. The money available through national assistance in no way compensates for the 'loss of face', the identity crisis, which is part of the pain of unemployment.

What then is the nature of this conflict that Jesus came to bring? It is in essence a radical shaking up of past conceptions, an awakening from the torpor of complacency to the facts of eternal life. His ministry brought the kingdom of God close to such people as were able to receive him and the gifts of the Holy Spirit that flowed from him. New life came to many who were afflicted in body and mind, so that they began to see what they might become if they only made themselves open to God. What mattered was not their antecedents but their openness to the future, rather like that of the publican in the famous parable. It was those who were proud that could not avail themselves of his grace, like his fellow citizens of Nazareth who could only associate him with his apparently insignificant background and were therefore both incredulous and jealous of his growing reputation. For such as these there was little conspicuous healing (Mark 6.1–6). The religious authorities were positively threatened by his charismatic powers, including his ability to discern hypocrisy masquerading as religious zeal, and it was they who conspired against him. When we read the terrible denunciation of the scribes and pharisees in Matthew 23, we must remember that the picture of Jewish piety was distinctly distorted by early Christian propaganda; converts have an unpleasant tendency to despise their spiritual roots as much out of unconscious guilt as conscious fervour. Nevertheless one can see how the authority of Jesus must have shocked and threatened the religious authorities on their own ground. And here is the conflict: between the old, well-tried ways of established tradition and the forward thrust of the Holy Spirit who is no respecter of persons, for God has no favourites (Acts 10.34–35). The same phenomenon occurred in the Christian Faith at the time of the Orthodox schism and even more radically with the Protestant reformation. In the latter particularly conflict has frequently boiled over into savage violence which has done the reputation of the Faith no little harm. As we have already seen, some of this fury has had psychopathological roots, but quite a share has been due to fear of being overwhelmed and destroyed by the opposing faction. Some of the trouble in Northern Ireland has this flavour, whether imaginary or real.

Where the Spirit of the Lord is, there is freedom (2 Corinthians 3.17), but who can claim the sole possession of the Holy Spirit? In the hands of the unlearned the Spirit can easily become a way of licence in which all past experience is sacrificed for the demands of the present moment. The guardians of the tradition have a vital role in seeing that charismatic activity is properly channelled to God's glory and the benefit of the people. Quite often, however, they try to gain control over the Spirit in the act of which they quench it. The corrupting property of power is a major theme throughout human history. It is implemented by the belief – indeed more a hope than a belief – that the truth lies in the possession of a single system of practice, and that any doubt is subversive sacrilege. The will to belief among humans is remarkable even in our very civilised age; it points to the basic insecurity that is part of their nature.

And so we may come back to the work of Jesus, the Prince of Peace who leaves a sword in his wake. One may first of all take two rather trite analogies, that of the dentist coping with a cavity in a patient's tooth and a surgeon dealing with an abscess or a malignant tumour. If the dentist were merely to apply a filling to close the cavity, the patient's relief would be short-lived. Instead there has first to be a complete excavation of the decay around the cavity, and only then can the defect be satisfactorily closed. Likewise a surgeon has to ensure a free draining of the pus contained within the abscess cavity before there can be proper healing; any residual pus will cause the condition to persist and even spread. In the same way it is essential that the entire tumour be excised if possible: any remnant will certainly grow and cause more trouble. In fact, if the condition cannot be completely cut away, the remnant is dealt with by radium therapy.

On a much vaster scale this principle has been at work throughout the twentieth century. It began, at least in Europe, with a plausible liberalism of thought derived from the evolutionary theories of

Charles Darwin and Herbert Spencer: civilisation was on the upgrade, and people were generally becoming kinder, more considerate to each other, and requiring the support of religion less and less. This last point was developed especially by the social critique of Karl Marx and the psychoanalytic dogma of Sigmund Freud. Both showed that with decent living conditions and proper family relationships religion would become increasingly a thing of the superstitious past. And then came the First World War, which shattered the illusions of evolutionary civilisation. The terrible eruption of violence among the principal warring powers, Germany, France and Britain, showed how superficial was the earlier liberalism, which in fact was a fiction of the European powers who maintained their position on a foundation of national supremacy and racial prejudice, usually implicit unless directly challenged.

After the rather uneasy truce of the twenties and the disastrous financial slump that followed there emerged a frankly racist regime in Germany that aimed not only at world domination but also total annihilation of the Jews, the traditionally alien group who prospered far too well for the comfort of the native population; the German church connived at much of this horror, being able to identify the present victims as representatives of those who were involved in the killing of Jesus. As we know, the Nazi horror culminated in the Second World War, at the end of which the previously despised national groups broke free of colonial rule and established their own sovereignty; the Jews too attained nationhood at the end of the scarcely believable Holocaust. Of even greater interest was the progress of the USSR, a conglomeration of states dedicated to the ideal of Marxist communism. Behind its facade of enlightened, antireligious humanism there lay a tyranny almost as noxious as that of Hitlerite Germany. Within very recent times the whole USSR complex has disintegrated due to economic collapse, a fit tribute to the idealistic folly of state socialism, and now a number of states have established their own autonomy.

When one compares the world situation at present with that before the First World War, the most striking difference is the coming of age of many people so that racism, although still prevalent, is now seen for the evil that it is. Likewise sexist discrimination is no longer acceptable (at least in theory) and a much more open attitude to deviant life-styles prevails, far preferable to the concealed ways of the past. But, alas, the horror of AIDS has followed closely on sexual liberation, both homosexual and heterosexual. Is the world a better place than it was before the First World War? The answer is a personal one: some things are better while others are worse (notably the ideal of service, which has now been largely replaced by selfish demands for comfort and privilege). What will the newly liberated states of the USSR do with their freedom? Will they act as wisely as the Western nations, now stripped of their imperial glory, and unite to form a common market, or will a fascist nationalism develop? To those of us who have seen much change in our lifetime, one thing is clear: human nature does not change. As St Paul said in Romans 7.22–23; 'In my inmost self I delight in the law of God, but I perceive in my outward actions a different law, fighting against the law that my mind approves, and making me a prisoner under the law of sin which controls my conduct.' He sees that God alone can rescue him from this state of death. His personal experience showed him that God acted through Jesus Christ, primarily on the road to Damascus but unremittingly thereafter.

Here we see the violence that Christ comes to bring. Just as St Paul was changed from being a pharisee who hated Christians to becoming the great Apostle to the Gentiles when he met Christ directly, so all of us have the chance of a similar transformation when we are completely open to God. The amazing series of events over the last ninety years have opened us to a possible encounter with God that the complacent intellectual liberalism of the early years of our century could never have done. And so, although human nature is unchanged, and the world a very threatening place, we are in a better condition to receive the full impact of Christ in our present uncertainty than ever before, when we were sure we knew all the answers.

He comes to change the face of humanity from a selfish one to one of generous self-giving. We do indeed lose our life (the *ego* self) willingly in the love of our neighbour, which is the whole creation. And then, the true life, the soul, emerges, and we know that eternity which embraces and changes all worldly concerns. But first, as I have just remarked, we need to be brought to our senses like the Prodigal Son as he set out to confront his father: he expected rejection but received burning love. One of the more enigmatic sayings of Jesus is this: 'Since John the Baptist came, up to the present time, the kingdom of heaven has been subjected to violence and the violent are taking it by storm' (Matthew 11.12). It might be the violence of Christ's love acting on those who had already repented of their sins under the cleansing influence of John's prior baptism. It is difficult for us to reconcile the peace of Christ's presence with the exertion necessary for us to attain that peace. But that is the way of creation: divine grace activating the will, so that the person plays his or her own part in the violence of the world around in order to bring tranquillity to that disorder.

It is evident that the Beatitudes are a prescription for the good life, but like most medical prescriptions, they need to be compounded by an expert. As Jesus would say; 'Things that are impossible for men are possible for God' (Luke 18.27). They are not within the scope of the unaided human will, because the *ego* gets in the way, demanding special privileges and mustering mortal violence if it unsatisfied. The violence of humans leads to destruction, whereas the violence of Christ brings to birth a new creation. And so, we do need the intermediary role of religious observance in our lives if we are to become fully actualised people.

It seems inevitable that conflict should dog our steps until we can learn to live with uncertainty, accepting that no human mind has all the answers. Once this adult acceptance comes to us, we can listen with courtesy to the views of other people, neither dismissing them as erroneous even before we have thought about them nor accepting them as the truth because of the rank or title of the person professing them. In other words, disagreement and diversity are of the very nature of reality as seen rationally, and, far from wanting everybody to fall in with our own views, we should actively encourage a range of opinions that may broaden our perspectives. In our very unstable world all this is a counsel of perfection. Most of us look for security in a changing, far from easy world. In fact the only security is the presence of God in our lives, and the violence of self-sacrifice is often necessary to allow that presence entry. Then will the Beatitudes become the way of civilised living.

Martin Israel is priest-in-charge of Holy Trinity, Prince Consort Road.

The churches in eastern Europe

Hugh Wybrew

FOR MOST PEOPLE in Britain, eastern Europe is a general area whose specific shape and borders do not spring instantly to their mental vision: I once had a letter addressed to me in Budapest, Romania. What we usually refer to as eastern Europe includes three distinct areas: the countries of the former Soviet Union; Poland, Hungary and Czechoslovakia, sometimes called Central Europe; and the south-east European countries of Romania, Bulgaria, and what was Yugoslavia. The one thing they had in common was government by communist regimes, and the one thing they have in common is the need to adjust to the collapse of communism in 1989. Each of these countries has its own specific political characteristics, and each has, too, its own Christian tradition. The problems therefore faced by the churches in eastern Europe vary, depending on the political, social and economic situation of their country, and on their own internal situation. It may help to review briefly which churches are where.

In the countries of the former Soviet Union which are Christian in tradition, the dominant church in Russia and Byelorussia is the Russian Orthodox Church. In the Ukraine three main churches compete: the Autonomous Ukrainian Orthodox Church (linked with the Moscow Patriarchate), the Ukrainian Catholic Church (a uniate church in communion with Rome) and the Autocephalous Orthodox Church (a national body not recognized by any other Orthodox Church). In Poland the dominant church is the Roman Catholic. Czechoslovakia and Hungary have Roman Catholic and reformed Churches. Romania is Orthodox, with Roman Catholic, Calvinist and Lutheran Churches among other ethnic groups in Transylvania, where there is also a Greek Catholic uniate Church embracing ethnic Romanians. Bulgaria is Orthodox, and Yugoslavia is divided: the Serbs, Macedonians, and Montenegrins are Orthodox, the Croats Roman Catholic, and Bosnia includes considerable minorities of

Orthodox Serbs and Catholic Croats alongside a large Muslim community of ethnic Serbs who converted after the Ottoman conquest. In all these countries there are of course smaller churches of other traditions, including Orthodox Churches in Poland, Czechoslovakia and Hungary, and Protestant Churches in Russia and Romania.

Under communist rule all religious organisations functioned under severe restrictions. Christian activities were confined to church buildings and educational institutions for the training of clergy. Most of what we regard as normal pastoral activity was impossible. Strenuous efforts were made to prevent Christianity infecting the young. All church life was under strict and detailed State supervision and control. The one exception to this general situation was perhaps the Roman Catholic Church in Poland, which as a church closely bound up with the life of the nation was sufficiently powerful to maintain a will and a voice of its own. But by and large the major churches had little option but to accept the situation and function as best they could within it. The Orthodox Churches had been accustomed since the fourth century to a close association with the State, and their sense of identity with the peoples whose national unity and culture they had often been instrumental in forming survived the transition from a Christian to a communist state. The Orthodox had no tradition of resistance to the State such as the Roman Catholics had, and owed no allegiance to a power beyond the reach of the communist authorities. Their situation, however, varied. The Russian Orthodox Church was probably the weakest, having suffered near extinction by 1939, limited revival under Stalin during and after the Second World War, and renewed persecution under his successors. The Romanian Orthodox Church was the strongest. It was never separated from the State, and was able to maintain a good educational system for the clergy, and a vigorous monastic life, albeit restricted by the State. The Roman Catholic Church in communist countries other than Poland was usually subjected to particular hardships, because of its links with the Vatican, and the Vatican's declared hostility to communism. So too were those of the Protestant Churches which resisted State interference and restrictions.

Since the collapse of communism in 1989 all churches in eastern Europe have found themselves free to manage their own affairs and engage in all forms of traditional pastoral activity. In the Soviet

Union church buildings and monasteries have been returned to the Orthodox Church at a rate of several a week. Churches which had been illegal have come out into open existence again, most notably the uniate churches in the Ukraine and Transylvania, which in 1946 and 1948 were forcibly reunited with the Russian and Romanian Orthodox Churches from which they had originally been persuaded into union with Rome. At the same time restrictions on religious activity originating outside the country have been lifted, and evangelists and sects of all kinds, mostly based in the USA, have poured into the former communist world. But as in the political realm, so in the religious, the immediate euphoria of 1989 has given way to a realisation that while there are undoubtedly immense new possibilities open to the churches, there are also considerable problems facing them.

A major difficulty is the lack of experience in many of the areas of pastoral work now open to the churches. For 40 years in most of these countries, and for 70 in the former USSR, the clergy have been unable to engage in pastoral visiting in homes, hospitals and prisons; they have been forbidden to teach religion to children under 18 either in schools or in church institutions. Their activity has been confined to the church building, and even there their preaching has been severely restricted to themes which could have no social or political application. The formation of the clergy needs to be broadened to include preparation for all these aspects of ministry. But there is a lack of teachers qualified to undertake such work. In some churches at least there is a lack of willingness among some of the clergy to take advantage of the new situation.

That is true also of some church leaders. In common with all others in positions of responsibility, high and low alike, Christian leaders in many of these countries learnt to do nothing without orders from above, for fear of stepping out of line. Now they find it difficult to accept responsibility, and to make the decisions necessary for taking advantage of the new freedom the churches enjoy. In addition many church leaders are seen by ordinary people as having been deeply compromised by their lack of resistance to communist manipulation, and their apparently willing compliance with government control. The Orthodox Patriarch of Romania resigned soon after the fall of Ceaucescu, ostensibly for reasons of

health, but in fact because he had incurred heavy criticism both
within and outside church circles for his unstinted praise of the
former President. But there was no senior hierarch who was less
compromised, and a few months later he was re-elected. It is difficult
for those outside to appreciate the kind of pressures to which church
leaders were subjected, and some of the criticism directed against
them in the West has failed to appreciate the realities of their situation, and the extent to which, within the limits of the possible, they
did their best to defend their churches; but it seems clear that within
the former communist countries there is often a need to renew
church leaderships if the churches are to win the respect of the
population at large.

That respect is not heightened by the divisions among the churches
which have in some cases been accentuated by freedom. In particular
relations between the Orthodox and Roman Catholic Churches have
deteriorated in the past two years, chiefly because of the legalisation
of the Ukrainian Catholic Church and the Greek Catholic Church
in Transylvania. In 1946 and 1948 their property passed to the Russian and Romanian Orthodox Churches, and the latter especially has
been reluctant to return church buildings and other property to the
uniates. But other issues too have contributed to the breakdown in
relations between Orthodox and Roman Catholics. In Russia and
elsewhere in the former communist countries the Orthodox accuse
Rome of seizing the opportunity presented by the collapse of communism to engage in missionary activity, designed to expand the latin-
rite Roman Catholic Church in areas traditionally Orthodox. Memories of former Roman aggression against the eastern Churches have
been revived, almost certainly not without reason. The Second Vatican Council spoke of the Orthodox as sister churches. But in the
former communist countries Roman Catholicism has been much less
influenced by that Council than in the West, and it had not generally
known the theological development which preceded and informed
the Council in western Europe and elsewhere. The new political
situation has enabled old rivalries and hostilities to break out into
fresh vigour.

There are signs that, paradoxical though it may seem, support for
the churches may have diminished since 1989. Throughout the period
of communist rule the churches – and other permitted religious

bodies – were the only organisations not directly controlled by the communist party. They became the focus for protest against communist regimes and the Marxist philosophy they imposed on their countries. For some years the Romanian government had exhorted young people not to go to church at Christmas and Easter. But they went, usually less for specifically religious reasons than to demonstrate their dissent from communist orthodoxy. Now the churches are no longer needed for that purpose: the days of rigid one-party rule are over, and dissent can be expressed in openly political form. Even in Poland there seems to have been a noticeable decline in popular support for the Roman Catholic Church. Candidates for the priesthood are fewer, and the numbers of people turning out for the last visit of the Pope were less than on previous occasions. There is widespread feeling, too, that the church is claiming too much power in the country's political life and in the personal life of its citizens. Quarrels over church property, too, are not calculated to enhance the church's moral authority among the faithful. It is said that in the Ukraine some four hundred parishes function outside the jurisdiction of any of the competing churches, with all of whose leaderships they are disillusioned.

All the traditional churches in the former communist countries are faced with the sudden invasion of a whole range of western evangelists, representing almost every conceivable sect, Christian, fringe Christian, or even non-Christian. Many of them are based in and financed from the United States of America, and some, like the Mormons, have set aside enormous sums of money for their missionary activities. They usually present a simple message, which can appear attractive to people disillusioned with the traditional church of their country. These sects present a powerful challenge to the traditional churches, and serve to fragment the Christian scene at a time when a united Christian front could make a valuable contribution to the rebuilding of former communist societies.

There is little doubt about the need for such rebuilding. Seventy, or even 45 years of communist rule has had a profoundly corrosive effect on the societies it oppressed. Such cohesion as they may have possessed before the advent of communism was dissolved under various pressures. Whatever idealism there may have been at the beginning of communist rule soon largely evaporated, as communism in practice became the arbitrary and despotic rule of the dominant élite within the leadership, imposed and maintained by force and in the Soviet Union and elsewhere at the cost of immense suffering and loss of life among ordinary people. In stark contrast with the socialist propaganda ceaselessly poured out by all the media, tightly controlled by the Party, the ruling class or *nomenklatura* enjoyed totally disproportionate economic privileges which protected them from the hardships experienced by most of the population. It is hardly surprising if one of the greatest problems facing most of these countries is that of re-establishing some measure of confidence in government among peoples who understandably regard all politicians with much cynicism. Few if any of these countries had a healthy political life before the advent of communism, to which they can look back and on whose sound traditions they can build. Established democratic traditions did not exist, except perhaps in Czechoslovakia, and even there they were of recent origin. Sound and viable political systems, as well as healthy societies, have to be constructed from the foundations upwards.

It was not only relations between governments and governed that suffered under communism. Social relations among the peoples themselves were deliberately undermined by the all-pervasive activities of the various security forces, such as the KGB in the Soviet Union or the notorious Securitate in Romania. Apart from the large numbers of people directly employed in such organisations, many others entered their service as informers, so that no one could be sure who was reporting to the security police on what they said and did. It might well be another member of their own family. In every block of flats, in every street, the security forces had their eyes and ears. It was the policy of divide and rule carried to such extremes that the normal relations of trust which bind the members of society together were almost fatally weakened. In addition, of course, there was the routine bugging of homes and tapping of telephones which impeded even normal communication among those of one's family and friends in whom one had confidence. The task of rebuilding societies undermined and fragmented in such ways is an enormous one. Trust in the State, and trust in one's fellow-citizens, need to be re-established if healthy societies are to emerge from the wreckage of communism. It will not be helped by the persistence of widespread corruption which communism did little to eradicate and usually helped to foster.

The harm done by communist regimes was not only political and social. It was also economic. Long before the political collapse of communism it had begun to fail economically. Almost from the beginning agriculture had been a disaster under the new socialist order. Productivity on State and collective farms was low, and the tiny plots left to the peasants produced a totally disproportionate amount of food. All communist governments felt obliged to pursue industrialisation. But the industries were often ill-conceived and poorly-sited, and produced goods of inferior quality. Centralised economic planning meant that industry was unresponsive to demand. Lack of resources in recent years, as economic decline intensified, meant that modernisation of industry could not take place. Not only is most industry in the former communist countries old-fashioned and inefficient, but it is also the cause of sometimes appalling pollution, with consequent extensive damage not only to human health but also to the natural environment. The extent of the problem with which the new governments are now confronted is well beyond their capacity to deal with, without massive and sustained economic assistance, both in terms of money and expertise, from the West. Shortage of basic necessities, rapid inflation, growing unemployment in societies where the very concept was unknown, the lack of adequate social-security provision in societies which at least in principle guaranteed full employment, have meant a serious fall in living standards for most of the eastern European countries. The apparent inability of the new governments to tackle these problems has diminished popular confidence in them, and caused some people to look back with regret to the old, communist, days.

At the same time the opening up of these countries to the West has enabled at least some people to profit from the economic situation of their country. Black market economies flourish. Anyone who can get hold of foreign currency can become rich. Years of socialist rule did not eradicate the universal human desire for money and material wealth. The end of communism has enabled it to come to the surface unchecked save by lack of opportunity. Some are willing to pursue any course that enables them to escape from poverty and shortages:

prostitution has come into the open as a flourishing industry in some of the big cities.

That is only one of the ways in which the moral rectitude which socialist regimes often imposed in their early days had already crumbled. The former communist countries had begun to suffer from all the social ills of the capitalist West long before the final disappearance of their regimes. Divorce and the breakdown of family life, drink and drugs, common crime – in all these respects socialist societies had come to resemble closely those of the West. Political freedom has done nothing to remedy them, and has only intensified the influences coming from the West, not excluding pornographic literature. Even before the changes of 1989 the Soviet Government had sought the help of the Russian Orthodox Church in combating the social problems besetting Soviet society. It may be wondered whether the churches of eastern Europe will be any more successful than those of the West in checking the influences of growing secularisation. While they may have profound influence on the individuals attracted into their membership, they are perhaps no more likely than their western counterparts to be able to influence the moral standards of the societies in which they live.

It may well be, in fact, that one of the greatest problems the churches in eastern Europe will have to face in the long run is secularisation and all that is associated with it. Persecution has enabled them to avoid facing some of the issues which have had a corrosive effect on Christianity in the West. Some of them, particularly those in the former Ottoman Empire and in Russia, lived in societies which were by-passed by the so-called 'Enlightenment' of the eighteenth century, and affected far less than western Europe by industrialisation in the nineteenth and early twentieth centuries. In predominantly agrarian societies the churches continued to occupy a traditional place in the life of most of the people. Only among the relatively small educated intelligentsia was religion questioned, and the practice of Christianity often abandoned. Under communist persecution all the churches had to concentrate on the main issue, of simply keeping faith in God alive as an alternative to official Marxist ideology. Now the stimulus to some sort of religious faith provided by communism has gone. It is likely that the intellectual questioning which has gone on inside as well as outside the churches in the

West will affect the churches in the East as well; and increasing urbanisation is likely to have a similar effect on religious practice as it has had in the West, and has already come to have, for example, in Romania. Religion in the East is likely to become more pluralistic, as traditionally dominant churches are joined by newer imports, and even by newer forms of religion. It has to be remembered, too, that although the churches in the East can claim the support of a far higher percentage of the population than those in the West, it is still only a minority of the population that adheres to any form of religion. The majority of the people in all the former communist countries does not, in any positive and active sense, believe in God.

It has become clear in the past two years that one of the most intractable problems facing both politicians and church leaders is nationalism. Communist regimes appeared to have kept under control the nationalist sentiments which had caused so much conflict, not least in south-east Europe, since the fall of the Ottoman and Austro-Hungarian Empires at the end of the First World War. They were in fact not always averse to making use of them for their own ends: Ceaucescu, for example, in Romania, made use of Romanian nationalism to reinforce his own power, and pursued a vigorous policy of Romanianisation among the Hungarian population in Transylvania. But in the last two years it has become abundantly clear that nationalism, where it appeared inactive, had been suppressed, not transcended. It has caused the dissolution of the former Soviet Union, and could lead to disastrous conflicts among its former constituent republics. It has already provoked violent conflict between Armenians and Azerbaijanis; and even within the Russian Federation itself there are stirrings among the minority ethnic groups incorporated into the Russian Empire long before the advent of communist power. Yugoslavia, too, held together since the end of the Second World War by the political will and personal power of Tito, has fallen apart into its constituent republics, and one of them, Bosnia, is in process of being torn apart by conflict among its three communities of Serbs, Croats and Muslims. Tensions exist between Czechs and Slovaks in Czechoslovakia, and Romanians and Hungarians in Transylvania; while in all countries of the former communist world there are minorities which engage the sympathies of neighbouring states to which ethnically they belong. Macedonia is one of the more complex national problems of south-east Europe, with claims and counter-claims being advanced by Bulgaria, Greece and Serbia, and by the Macedonians themselves. One of the causes of the Balkan Wars at the beginning of the century, it could emerge again as a source of conflict and violence. It will be long before the peoples of eastern Europe work through their sometimes fierce sense of national identity, to achieve a mutual tolerance and will to cooperation beyond the present tensions and conflicts.

The Christian churches do not always stand apart from nationalism. In the conflict between Serbia and Croatia part of the problem lies in their different Christian traditions. The Croats have been part of Catholic central Europe for a thousand years, the Serbs part of the Orthodox world. During the centuries in which they were subject to Muslim Ottoman rule, it was the Orthodox Church which kept alive the Serbs' sense of national identity. Even when church leaders recognise the need for their communities to work for reconciliation and the healing of memories, it is not easy to distinguish church from people when the two have been so closely bound together for so long. The Orthodox Church in particular has come to be organised on national lines, so that national independence brings with it pressure for an independent church. It is likely that the Moscow Patriarchate will be forced to grant independence to the Orthodox Church in the Ukraine, at present still dependent on the Russian Orthodox Church. But no less strong an association binds the Roman Catholic Church to Polish history and national identity. Such historic links between church and nation can have negative consequences for minority churches within those nations. There is too the less healthy association, not unknown in the West either, of extreme right-wing political groups which make use of religion to support their nationalist aims. These can sometimes be anti-semitic in outlook as well, compounding their harmful influence. Religion can sometimes be part of the problem it should ideally be helpful in resolving.

The peoples of the former communist world are faced with formidable problems. They must construct viable political systems which will ensure them basic personal, civic and religious freedom. They must rebuild their failed economies and fragmented societies. They must come to terms with the national sentiments and rights of others. Most of them live within a national and cultural tradition formed by

Christianity. It is a Christianity itself divided, Catholic, Orthodox, Protestant, often nationalist in character, and with its own internal problems. The western influences to which their world is now completely open are not always helpful, and the motives of western governments not always as disinterested as they might be. Yet, the success or failure of these peoples in confronting the immense task of reconstruction is of immediate concern to western Europe. They need all the help they can be given.

Hugh Wybrew is vicar of St Mary Magdalen's, Oxford. He was formerly Secretary of the Fellowship of St Alban and St Sergius and Dean of St George's Cathedral, Jerusalem.

'Forgive us our debts . . .'

A Personal Plea

'IT'S A RECESSION', the banks tell us, 'and we are losing money.' Those insomniac enough to catch the 6 am business news are greeted at regular, normally six-monthly, intervals with the horrifying details of how yet another high-street name announces catastrophic losses equalling the Gross Domestic Product of many a small country, only to watch its share price jump up at the news.

Why should bank shares jump so? Why are pennies added to prices while profits sink? The reason is simple: the banks are in fact making, as banks have always made, pots of money. The secret to making a loss whilst hiking up your share price is 'provisions'. The losses are inverted by using massive profits to cover Third-World debts which are not being repaid. Thus you inspire the confidence of your peers that you are a solid and powerful institution and in return they buy your shares.

Such has been the banks' alacrity in tucking away these billion-pound nest-eggs that many banks are now approaching 100 per cent cover of the 'bad debts' which they are owed by Third-World countries. More recent 'provisions' are now being made to cover loans made in the late 1980s to open small businesses like your local Futon Shop (you know, the one with 'Everything Must Go' in its window).

Cheered by this news of 100 per cent cover the happy Christian, or anyone who lives his or her life by a moral code whether Islamic or atheist, says, 'Wonderful, we can now forgive and forget those foolishly and greedily made loans and allow these poor countries to operate free of their burden.' Unfortunately, it appears that the banks' only concession to a moral code is the act of closing at weekends. Debt is big money. Watch carefully!

When you put your money into a bank, the bank is pleased because it can use your money to lend far more money to others at a higher interest rate than it pays you. Thus the bank earns pots of money, and pays you a little of it. The deposit that you make can be recalled at any time by visiting the bank and withdrawing your money – thus the bank sees your nest egg as a liability which it will have to repay. The loan which the bank makes on the strength of your deposit is its true asset, bearing high interest and subject to recall or foreclosure if the borrower defaults.

Billions of dollars were lent to the Third World during the 1970s, bearing interest and capital repayments which crippled the countries who had borrowed. The banks were desperate to lend to countries, since the common wisdom had it that a country never defaulted and never went bust. In the 1980s several countries, in particular Latin American countries, defaulted. A swift lesson for the banks went as follows: a country can default on a bank, but a bank cannot foreclose on a country. The loans made could not be enforced, these 'assets' could not be realised. They appeared to be worthless. Note the word 'appeared'.

Bankers, particularly merchant bankers, are on occasion an optimistic bunch; what is a bull market except the triumph of optimism over evidence? It was in the back of their minds that some debts might eventually be repaid and this glimmer of hope gave the assets a value. Not much of a value, perhaps only 10 per cent of the full amount of the loan, but it was something. More excitingly, as the glimmer of hope rose and dimmed with political and economic changes, so the value went up and down. As any merchant-banking schoolboy will tell you, an easily transferable commodity with a fluctuating value over time, together with decent guesswork, is all you need to make a buck. You could buy $100 million of Latin-American debt at 10 cents on the dollar, sell it at 11 cents and make a cool million. The party started and within a few years all the major merchant banks had an 'asset trading' division. Why forgive the debt when it is so profitable?

Then comes the next variant. Suppose you want to build a mill to pulp and turn into paper the rainforest which the Latin Americans sell to you in a desperate bid for hard currency? The mill might cost $100 million to construct. But why pay so much? You can buy $100 million of debt for 10 cents on the dollar, so pay out $10 million for that. Then go to the government and say, 'Give me $100 million in your own currency, rather than the dollars which I previously required, and we will call it quits. I will then build my pulping mill in the rainforest with the money. I gain a mill, you gain jobs and infra-structure and repay debt. All you have to do is print the money.'

This is described as a virtuous circle. So far, so sophistically good. But that schoolboy in the merchant bank will tell you what printing money creates in an economy: inflation. In countries already blowing up with hyperinflation, for which the poor and starving pay with their lives, more money was printed with which to line the pockets of contractors and investors. The banks took, take, commissions for these 'debt into equity' deals. What is two per cent of $100 million? Ring it up. Who cares about inflation? If you have a dollar bank account, you can sit it out.

To their credit, the bankers imagine they are doing good with their deals. They make money, allow repayment in home currencies and create jobs. It is as well for them to ignore the destruction of the rainforest by countries to earn hard currency which they can no longer borrow. It is as well for them to ignore the child forced to choose between prostitution and starvation because the price of bread has doubled overnight. The bankers think that they have found the secret of the free lunch – that everybody wins. The forest dweller who loses his world and the child forced to leave a home that cannot feed him tell us most eloquently: there is no such thing as a free lunch.

Lately, a far more effective deal has been struck between banks to profit from Latin America. Again it involves the clever manipulation of debt but this time in doing so pushes banking to the very limits of the line between sharp practice and illegality. It is a deal which is little more than a confidence trick. It can only be outlined in the most basic and simplified way and no doubt it has greater subtleties than can be expressed here, but it is a scam based on these principles and practised in the City of London.

In order to show good faith, certain Latin American countries earmarked certain of their debts and said to the western banks: 'You may have these debts repaid in hard dollars, rather than our local currency. Our condition for this repayment is that the dollars must be somehow re-invested in our economy or at least dedicated for re-investment within 28 days or else be re-deposited with us.' This put up the value of that debt to, say, 50 cents in the dollar, the discount being for the strict 're-invest and re-deposit' stipulation.

An enormous carrot was being held out to the banks, who eyed it greedily. You could get your hands on the dollars; the hard currency earned by making Volkswagen Beetles; cutting down trees and selling beef could be yours. All you had to do was to find a way not to re-pay it. Your own massive exposure to that country (it still owes you billions and could get very shirty if you renege on the stipulation) together with your desire to maintain your good name and not be blackballed from your clubs, means that you have to find a third party.

Quickly, you buy $100 million of the special debt for $50 million. You find an obscure third-party bank with no connection with the relevant country. You persuade the bank to assume the obligation to re-deposit and pay it $10 million for its trouble. Then you cash in your bond. The Central Bank of the relevant country pays you $100 million in hard dollars and waits for it to be invested or re-deposited. You pay the agreed $10 million to the third party and run the rest, $40 million, through a series of shell banks throughout the world to hide your involvement.

You have made a fortune and when the Central Bank goes to the third party to ask for a re-deposit there is no reply or, at least, no money to re-deposit at all. Thus that country is deprived of the hard currency so hard won. Such deals were being perpetrated as recently as 1991. They may still be – details are hard to come by for reasons which will be obvious. It may be that Central Banks are now wise to the scam. Let us hope so.

The only way to avoid the inevitable destruction of life and the environment which is caused by the North-South global divide of wealth and poverty is to allow the South to prosper. No country can prosper when it is both crushed by debt and bled of its resources.

In the *Pater Noster* Christians plead, 'Dimitte nobis debita nostra' – 'forgive us our debts'. We must forgive them theirs.

The anonymous author of this article is a lawyer who was for a number of years involved in Third-World finance.

Morality in a society without an agreed system of values

Peter Pilkington

HISTORICALLY most human societies have possessed an ideology which embodied the principal moral ideas prevalent in that society. Often these ideologies were supported by religious systems. Edmund Leach, an agnostic anthropologist, wrote: 'The most important thing about religion is that it provides the believer with an ideology – a world view about how I am related to the world around me and how parts of the world are related to one another.' Religious ideologies presented their moral principles as an ordered set of rules placed within the context of an orderly universe. Edmund Leach in the same lecture suggested that human beings seem to need such an orderly system as it appears that we are not simply concerned with imposing order upon nature, we also need to impose order on our own behaviour; we need to make moral distinctions. If we lack confidence in our ability to recognise clear-cut boundaries, it would not just be a matter of arguing whether the seashore was part of the land or sea, or whether whales should be rated as fish, the issue would be far more worrying and personal in that it would involve the means by which we distinguish between clean and unclean, right and wrong. In the past societies had their systems which were reflected in their religious and moral structures. In western Europe no such system exists in that those of the past have either broken down or are very weak. It is possible that we are the first society in history to experience this phenomenon and even now we are not sure of our situation since it is only recently that the full effects of this process can be felt. Our generation does not have an agreed system of values and insecurity and uncertainty result from this development.

The nineteenth century witnessed a decline in organised religion. Rapid industrialisation and the emergence of great cities weakened the link between Church and people, in spite of the heroic efforts of many devoted priests and ministers. Further, the great biblical symbols lost their force when translated into the impersonal world of the new industrial towns. Those vivid themes of conflict between herdsman and farmer, parables like that of the lost sheep, the symbols of bread and water, so clear to our rural ancestors, meant little to the factory worker or suburban householder. The great moral lessons underlying the myths and stories of the Old Testament as well as the revelations of the New were lost as scholars were only concerned with asking questions of date, origin and truth. A society was created which increasingly lost touch with the roots and source of its religious ideology and morals.

Yet many intellectuals of the late nineteenth century felt that even in an atmosphere of religious doubt or indifference it was possible to maintain an agreed pattern of cultural, intellectual and moral ideals which could influence and even transform society. In a strange way, the determinist and secularist philosophy of Marx was an attempt to provide a moral ideology for this non-believing and affluent society. Matthew Arnold illustrated another reaction in that though he lacked religious certainty he still felt that there was an agreed pattern of cultural and intellectual ideals which could guide and model society. The aim of culture is to ascertain what perfection is and to make it prevail. It is similar to religion but greater – it is a harmonious expansion of all the powers that make the beauty and worth of human nature. Thus culture goes beyond religions as generally conceived by us. More than this it is a social idea: 'the men of culture are the true apostles of equality.' Thus, in a society which had lost many of the certainties of religion, 'Matthew Arnold still had confidence in an agreed culture which could sustain an agreed moral framework.

Arnold's ideal demanded considerable culture and sophistication and it is hard to see its values influencing the more deprived sections of society. It was a culture and ethic for the elite and paid little regard to the vast changes that had occurred in society as a result of industrialisation. Further, even as Matthew Arnold wrote, common patterns of culture and belief were being questioned. One hundred years of romanticism had weakened the Renaissance rules of perspective, style and proportion. Romantic individualism and self-expression combined with a questioning of established attitudes have

governed the cultural scene over the last hundred years. Art, literature, music and architecture all bear witness to the lack of an agreed
set of cultural values. English teachers disagree as to what constitutes
an elegant style, art critics argue over what constitutes true art –
subjectivity and self-expression govern the creative arts. Even if we
share Arnold's view of the power of culture to refine, we cannot
agree on what is refining culture. Neither Marxism nor secular intellectual culture have succeeded in filling the vacuum created by the
collapse of the traditional Christian ideology.

Increasingly, individualism combined with the removal of restrictions on an individual's self-realisation have decided the thinking of
our society. As far as possible each person should be judged on his
own values and not be restricted by any objective standards. Our
nineteenth-century ancestors were sufficiently confident in their
moral values and prepared us to be ready to impose them on other
cultures. In India they made *suttee* illegal but today many would
question their right to make such a judgement on another civilisation.
Relativism and individualism govern the moral scene.

In such a climate it is not surprising that there is no agreed system
of morality. The life-styles of our society are so various and ever-
changing that it is almost ludicrous to talk of a common pattern. All
the deeper issues of human life are the subject of conflict – marriage,
abortion, sexuality, religious instruction, discipline, and patterns of
education all are battlefields for differing ideologies. These struggles
create an atmosphere of tension and doubt which is in part the cause
of the deep problems which characterise adolescence in many parts
of the western world.

In this society without an agreed system of morality, and in an
atmosphere of cultural relativism, some have tried to find an answer
in a pragmatic and practical approach. Our age could truly be called
the age of technique. No longer do we talk about moral rules which
demand our adherence and to which we must submit our personal-
ities. Books and magazines tell us of techniques and skills which can
create relationships, produce happy marriages, and secure children.
They even tell us how to be successful in business or how to manipu-
late others. There is no agreed pattern and therefore we must acquire
skills to survive in this complex and competitive world without rules

or values. 'Life skills' is now a popular course in many schools and while it has some virtues, the emphasis is on skills rather than values.

Yet, all history shows us that we need more than this and that without some form of moral order we become confused and insecure. Certainly our society presents many examples of tension and uncertainty. Life-long marriage has become increasingly difficult to sustain, adolescence is often a scene of anxiety and tension, and old age is seen as a fearful burden in a society that places such value on success and beauty.

The Church has found it hard to know how to react to this secular and insecure society. All churches have shown a tendency to abandon the strong moral positions of the past. The reasons for this are complex and at least in part show religious institutions reflecting the developments in society as a whole. The theories of psycho-analysis that human behaviour was often influenced by sub-conscious feelings had a profound effect on moral behaviour and discipline. It was felt that many of the moral disciplines of the past resulted from a defensive insecurity and crushed rather than assisted the development of human personality. The largely existentialist thrust of much modern theology, emphasising personal commitment, strengthened this feeling that moral behaviour ought to result from personal choice rather than submission to external rules. Marxist determinism with its emphasis on economic forces governing human behaviour also affected some churchmen who felt it wrong to enforce strict moral codes on the poor, when at least in part their sins resulted from deprivation. Some theologians felt it was wrong to condemn sexual activity outside marriage if there was personal commitment and acceptance. Similarly, traditional church rules banning physical homosexual acts were abandoned and again it was argued that as there was personal commitment and love this more reflected the spirit of the gospel than external restrictions. Individualism and self-expression have come to influence large areas of the Church's teaching just as they have in the rest of the community. The Church of England, because of its divisions and its lack of any strong authority, has experienced these conflicts and perplexities more deeply than many other denominations.

Yet, if we turn to the gospel, we find our Lord saying that he came not to destroy but fulfil the Law. It is true that the gospels and epistles are full of attacks on the aridity and hypocrisy of the Law, as laying down rules which affect outward behaviour but not the heart. The whole essence of St Paul's teaching is that goodness must spring from grace, and cannot be induced by external rules, yet it is a caricature of this teaching to argue that it means the abandonment of strong moral codes as he himself stresses. Our Lord shows compassion and acceptance to the woman taken in adultery but tells her to go and sin no more. Our Lord shows acceptance and love for Zacchaeus the tax collector when he asks him to dinner, but we are told that the response of Zacchaeus was to give away his ill-gotten gains. Sin is conquered by love not by rules but there is no abandonment of rules of morality. Since the time of our Lord the essence of Christianity has been that the fact of faith is translated into a life of disciplined service. The Church can be compassionate to the sinner but need not condone the sin.

If Christianity is to bear true witness to our Lord in our present society, it is crucial that it maintain its traditional moral demands without hypocrisy or harshness. Only in doing this can we free our society from that deep insecurity which results from moral uncertainty and lack of boundaries. We must not feel guilty at making moral demands on our world. Nor must we abandon our Christian duty to discipline ourselves. This was once one of the great strengths of the Catholic movement in our Church and must be recognised if we are to maintain our moral integrity and vision.

The Church has too easily surrendered to the prevailing view of our society that it is impossible, even wrong, to maintain the traditional Christian morality. In part, its position has been weakened by the massive attacks that have been made on the authority of biblical revelation over the past two hundred years. The greatest problems have arisen from scholars like Bultmann questioning the nature of the incarnation which lies at the very heart of the Christian faith. In *Kerygma and Myth* Bultmann saw much of the New Testament as myth and reduced the resurrection to a subjective faith experience. Inevitably, this has affected the authority of the moral teaching of our Lord and the early Church. It is felt that society has undergone such enormous changes that we need to find a new system of moral values just as we need a new theology. It is argued that the patterns of the past no longer reflect the realities of modern society.

In face of contraception, greater expectations, and the nature of current morality it is impossible to demand chastity before marriage, life long commitment to one partner, and many other aspects of the former morality. We must accept the changes and look for integrity in relationships even though they break the moral rules of the past. The problem is that such a pattern of morality lays an enormous burden on the individual and certainly does not produce the psychic security that many human beings require. Just as Matthew Arnold's ideal of cultural and intellectual ideals guiding society demanded clever and sophisticated individuals, so does this very personal morality. It is an ideal that only seems to prosper within an affluent and cultivated circle, and even there tensions can occur. The prevalence of divorce has caused problems at all levels of society but again they are most acute amongst the more deprived. It is arguable that more problems result from the collapse of the traditional family than from poverty, yet the Church is more ready to see poverty as the main enemy than the fact of easy divorce. This is not to argue that the Church should not protest against injustice or argue for help for the deprived of our society, but it must not at the same time abandon its support for traditional moral values. The Church must resist the temptation to escape the dilemmas of guiding personal morality by dictating moral patterns to the State. The problems of our society cannot be solved merely by laying our moral burdens on the State. The whole experience of eastern Europe has shown that egalitarianism or State morality still leaves many moral problems.

In the end Christianity is about our response to the will of God as revealed in the incarnation of our Lord. In its 2000 years of history the Church has often opposed the patterns of existing societies because of the commandments of Christ. It has forgiven the sinner without accepting the sin. It is dangerous for us to argue that because we have no agreed system of values we cannot any longer make the moral demands of the past. If Christian history shows anything it is that these demands ennobled rather than destroyed the individual.

Peter Pilkington is a canon emeritus of Canterbury, former High Master of St Paul's School, and at present Chairman of the Broadcasting Complaints Commission and a member of the Parole Board.

Here I stand!

Norry McCurry

I START by recounting four incidents all of which have something in common. They occurred in the 1960s '70s, and '90s.

First, a television programme in the days of black and white. A group of well known people, Dilys Powell, Robert Boothby and John Betjeman, are seen having dinner and talking animatedly to each other. The conversation is quick, amusing, informed, and you are made to feel that you are at the table too and Bob Boothby will give you a conspiratorial smile. They know the great and the good, they take it for granted that traditional standards are dated and absurd (this is 30 years ago, remember). Dilys Powell brings the conversation around to divorce. 'Of course,' she says, 'everyone feels today it is positively healthy to start on a second marriage if the first breaks down, don't we, John?' Betjeman looks down at the empty wine glass. 'Oh no, I'm afraid I don't agree at all,' he says sadly. You feel he has broken the rules of the game, he is guilty of bad taste, the producer will be having fits. There is an embarrassed pause around the table. The fact is that John Betjeman has taken a moral stand.

Now we are in the 1970s and the setting is a parish in east London. There are many ways of making life more bearable in a borough where there are more children in care than anywhere else in England. Bishop Trevor Huddleston has written to *The Times* after a child is found drowned in a canal that runs through the parish and Janet, a practising member of the local church sets up a Canoe Club for youngsters with the bishop's encouragement. She has had to battle with no less than five different authorities over two years to get this project launched, and in a group of community workers and youth leaders who share the same ideals she is a popular figure. They meet in the same pub. One night it becomes clear that they expect her to join them in pressurising the Area Health Authority to open a clinic for abortion on demand. Janet refuses to sign the petition and everyone is startled, even dismayed. It would be different, she fancies they are thinking, if she were a Catholic, but she's Church of England. Oh well, it's all very odd. If she were a less strong woman Janet would feel isolated.

The third incident occurred the other day. Anne in her late twenties teaches in a girls' secondary school. She has travelled in India, goes regularly to Taizé, is high spirited and popular. She belongs to Amnesty, is vegetarian and belongs to her Union. She seldom goes on demonstrations and is not highly political but she stands by what she believes are enlightened ideas. Anne found herself at a party given by the friend of a friend where the young women were wearing extremely smart dresses and the young men had had, she reckons, expensive haircuts. Anne doesn't always think before speaking and soon she made some remark about the rights of gay people and how they should be encouraged to 'come out'. She was instantly aware that such remarks are socially unacceptable, people raised their eyebrows and moved away. And Anne was left reflecting that she must be moving in circles where people of her age share the same standards and that it's time she became aware of the rest of society.

All these stories suggest to me that if certain principles matter deeply to us then we must be prepared to stand up for them. Sometimes, too, we need to choose whether some are more important than others. A priest whose task was to select candidates for the ministry used to startle students who felt they had a direct line to God by suddenly asking them 'What ditch would you choose to die in?'

If I choose a particular issue to defend with passion it may be due to the part it has played in my background. Readers of *The Tablet* will recognise that many Roman Catholics see the Pope as leading the world in pleading for human rights and condemning war, while maintaining a far from progressive stance on the position of women in the Church. This, it is generally felt, may have a connection with his upbringing in Poland. And those of us who have profited from a Myers Briggs Personality assessment week-end will realise that, because of our personality traits, we are likely to espouse certain causes or not and that some who hold deep seated beliefs may find it harder than other people do to stand up and be counted. So it may be that we have never thought through the rights and wrongs of something controversial like euthanasia. It seems so complicated that we hesitate about being too dogmatic until it knocks on our door.

Jeremy's wife contracted Altzheimer's Disease becoming progressively helpless and in the end terribly ill. She lay there, he said later, panting like a dog and all he was able to do was to give her sips of water. Her pitiable condition and his grief became the subject of concern to doctor and nurses. 'Would you,' they asked, 'agree if we gave her something to calm her down?' 'Oh, yes *please*,' he replied. So they did. His wife became much calmer, and then strangely still. She was dead. Jeremy was left with a tormenting sense of guilt. Had he really colluded in the killing of his beloved one?

During the course of war service people were faced with unexpected choices. My ship, a frigate, had dropped astern of the convoy we were escorting – asking the procession of ships to sail on towards Gibraltar while we with engines silent hovered on a spot where we believed a German U-boat was lying deep below us quite still. We scarcely spoke. Suddenly the captain said loudly: 'I intend that when they surface we'll show them no mercy. Not after all the innocent lives they've taken. I'll shoot them there and then.' None of us was prepared for this decision. What if the submarine were to rise slowly to the surface and German sailors were seen climbing out of the conning tower, arms upraised in surrender, what was one to do? Seize the pistol out of the captain's hand?

It is time that we moved on to see how in so many ways people's attitudes to what is right and wrong have changed. Let me ask you to consider certain assumptions that held good in the past and became gradually questioned and abandoned. It seems to me evident that some of the inherited assumptions in our society have changed and most, if not all, changes have been for the better. It is often held that in many areas the Church has dragged its feet and reluctantly followed public opinion. But there are also signs that Christianity has encouraged change and progress.

Perhaps in the past it was a simple world inasmuch as everyone had a place in society assigned to them according to where they were born – assigned by those who dominated society and who moulded public opinion. So the poor had their place. Nothing makes this more clear than the verse in that most popular of all children's hymns written by Mrs Alexander, *All things bright and beautiful.*

> The rich man in his castle,
> The poor man at the gate.
> God made them high or lowly,
> And ordered their estate.

But not only the poor. Women too had their place. In both these examples there was something ultimate; it was not to be questioned. After all the bible sanctioned it and the law enforced it. As for black people, they certainly had their place. For they were not like us, not like us at all.

In the nineteenth century we see stirrings. Dickens uses his novels to show his sense of passionate outrage that the social system allowed the poor to suffer, allowed children to go begging in bare feet (in Belfast while I was growing up barefooted children sold newspapers on street corners). Dickens was angry because no one troubled to notice their sufferings or do anything about it. Wilberforce in his campaign against slavery brought a change of attitude in parliament, and Shaftesbury led a long and slow movement to reform the prison service.

Josephine Butler was challenging popular opinion and inherited assumptions. She insisted that women forced through poverty into prostitution should never be spoken of as bad women. Shaw in *Mrs Warren's Profession* said of a middle-class woman that if this was the only way she could earn a living she was not to be condemned. George Eliot, in *Adam Bede* introduced her readers to The Preacher, a woman determined to lead the life she believed God was calling her to regardless of the consequences. And in *Middlemarch* she gave us Dorothea – a far more penetrating portrayal of a modern woman than the English had ever read of before.

Such writers, such politicians enabled people to discover that there is another side from the one taken for granted about women. Women were seen actually to have feelings – feelings very different from the pitiful, sentimental portrayal of *Little Dorrit* and equally different from that found in the witty, decadent dialogue of Restoration comedies. There was a dawning awareness that people born without privilege suffered in a manner which meant that no one could go on accepting as right the place assigned to them by society. Inherited beliefs began to crumble because they were being increasingly questioned.

Another cause of this change was the effect of democracy. It is a very different world in Britain, however much disparity still remains, now that women have the vote and people with no property have the vote and black people have the vote. Everyone may talk about what is right and what is wrong and make moral decisions. Are people free to take a stand if they belong to a different class in society from John Betjeman or Janet or young Anne? It seems to me their choice is either to challenge the status quo or collude with it.

Suppose you are a person obliged to live in a squalid block of council flats where the smell of urine is never absent from the lifts and the windows below are boarded up. Suppose you are a West Indian who sees evidence every day that he is being discriminated against – then perhaps you will feel you are faced with such a choice.

Those who challenge, who say, 'Here I stand. I will not be treated like this,' will find themselves looked on as trouble makers. The Ministry of Defence became increasingly hostile to the women of Greenham Common. Black people who struggle for racial justice are not venerated as is Martin Luther King, they are treated as wearisome by the authorities. Women who campaign to be taken seriously and listened to as women are written off as strident.

So you are faced with a choice. Either you can say, 'I have made my decision. I refuse to give in to the assumptions of a society which holds me down because of my sex or the colour of my skin,'; or else you can decide that it will be easier if you submit and act out the role you have been given in this play. So you may stifle your longing for justice, for it will only bring down nastiness on your head. Moses who challenged the status quo experienced this very thing first from Pharaoh and then from his own people who turned against him when he had led them out of slavery. So you end up colluding. Thus it is that some women and some black people who feel the injustice but stifle themselves and refrain from protesting, end by becoming the keenest supporters of the dominating point of view.

An important example of this is the position in England today of gay people. There is, of course, an inherited and generally accepted view of homosexuals which is backed up by a superficial glance at the Bible. People by and large feel they really do not want to know, because deep down they are disturbed that such people exist. A minority feel downright hostile or suspicious while an increasing number of people feel that gay people should keep their sexuality out of sight. Alas that the Church is so ambivalent on the subject. One outspoken critic on record says:

It is quite extraordinary that in the Church of England we all talk as if homosexuals were other people 'out there'. The climate is such that homosexuals are all reduced to silence because of fear of speaking out. It is a tragic breach of charity that members of our Church should be reduced to this. We have a duty to listen carefully to them.[1]

What is the moral decision open to a gay person in this situation? Some have stopped concealing it. They say; 'I do not believe this to be right. It does not feel right. I have a vote like everyone else and I believe I exist as I am.' This was the step taken by Michael Peet, Team Rector of Bow, when he spoke in *The Times* last year with complete honesty about himself and his partner in the course of a long interview. But most people feel reticent about courting publicity in this way because of the risks involved.

We are faced with a choice between three approaches. We may try to look at it if we can from God's point of view. We can look at it from the traditional point of view (it is wrong, it feels distasteful, we would prefer not to know about it) or we can look at it from the point of view of the people themselves (I don't feel a sinner, I don't believe I should be an outcast, I believe myself to be loved by God as I am). If we take the view that it is a person's own attitude to what he/she *is* that needs to be at any rate *listened* to, then we are feeling our way to the third approach. We need to see the work of Jesus as challenging the way we pigeon-hole people. We would not behave in this way towards people we love. We have got to recognise that we are all sisters and brothers under the skin.

So Mrs Alexander was wrong on all fronts. For on each of these examples there is absolutely nothing of *God* in the places and roles which society has assigned to them. We must be on our guard against

ever colluding in keeping them in those places. It is our common
humanity which counts. It is this which transcends our social position,
the colour of our skin and our sexual orientation. The point I am
making is this. Wherever in recent history we see change taking
place which is change for the good, it seems to be the sort of change
Jesus came to bring. That poor people should not stay poor, that
other races should not be regarded as inferior to us. These are the
changes which I see to be the work of God. One can, I believe, see
them as the result of centuries of Christianity.

But what authority do we look to in coming to decisions which
are moral decisions? Many people are looking for authority, but
where does authority lie? – in the Church? In Scripture? In our own
experience? As an ordinand, in 1941, I remember going out and
buying a set of four volumes on moral theology by a Jesuit called
Davies. Davies S. J. had it all there, His was the confessor's manual
and you knew where you were when faced with any moral dilemma.
I remember the guidelines on matters sexual were kept in Latin! But
the days of Davies S. J. are long past. Alistair MacIntyre puts it this
way:

There seems to be no rational way of securing moral agreement . . . the
most striking feature of contemporary moral utterance is that so much of it
is used to express disagreement.[2]

So where are we? Walter Briueggermann, the American Biblical
scholar, insists that we are in a state of transition. This has been
identified as the transition to a pluralist society, the transition to a
secular society and a transition to a world economy.[3] You might say
therefore that we are on shifting sands, holding out our hand for the
hand of God to grasp it. Are we then left with conscience? P. D.
James in her novel *Devices and Desires* has a woman who cannot
see her way through a moral dilemma seeking the advice of a clergy-
man who tells her that ultimately she must listen to her conscience,
for it is through our conscience that God speaks. 'But how,' she
asks, 'can I be certain that it is *God* speaking?'

We are not to regard ourselves simply as individuals going our
own way and making our own choices. We belong to the community
of the people of God. So the authority of the Church weighs heavily

upon us. How are we going to approach this? Nicholas Holtam who ministers to his people on the Isle of Dogs learns much from them and is aware that there is a great deal of love around. But he is also aware of a wide gulf between the orthodox Christian teaching that governs relationships and what actually is to be found in people's lives. This 'great gulf' is not confined to the Isle of Dogs; what the Church lays down has little connection with many people's sexual standards in all classes of society.

Might we find a way through if we treated all this in aesthetic rather than legalistic terms? It has been suggested that we can describe it in terms of painting and show how one artist will follow the rules while another will breach the rules and yet expand our imagination. Simply to go by the rules as certain guide books in moral decision-making suggest is wooden and lifeless, like painting by numbers!

To test this out I went to the Sainsbury Wing of the National Gallery where Paula Rego, the first of the Gallery's associated artists, had an exhibition. Paula Rego feels herself to be in the basement, with the great pictures above.

I was very scared and a bit daunted. But to find one's own way anywhere one has to find one's own door, just like Alice, you see. You've got to find your own doorway into things and I thought the only way you can get into things is through the basement which is exactly where my studio is, in the basement.[4]

She goes upstairs to the great masters and brings ideas down and munches away at them.

Her work is very exciting. Taking a seventeenth-century painting by Philippe de Champaigne of St Joseph asleep with the angel appearing to him in vision, while our Lady looks on, she found herself painting an elderly man heavily asleep in an armchair – flat out – while a young woman whose backside bulges out on a camp stool draws him with great concentration. Above is a drawing of her guardian angel who is so real he appears to be leaping from the easel. Alongside this painting Paula Rego has the same man, retired and looking ten years younger quietly enjoying mementoes of his travels round the world, while a girl of 10 draws beside him something which she is hiding from our view.

These two pictures stir the imagination invoking many of one's own experiences. I myself used to be a sailor. I too am getting old. I have a daughter who is dear to me. I too look back and the young give me pleasure. Paula Rego's world is strange and I am not quite sure where I am in it. But her paintings of the Visitation and of Martha and Mary, permanently displayed in the Sainsbury Wing Restaurant are riveting and unconventional. So these works conveyed something to me which the famous Old Master did not and I feel like saying, 'Yes, they make sense, they are somehow true, they have widened my vision and I am at home with them.'

This, I must stress, is not to say that our decision making is to be purely instinctive. We need the Scriptures and we need the Church if we are not to be loners. But isolated extracts from the Bible may certainly not be regarded as a timeless moral code and New Testament ethics must be understood in their historical context: only think of slavery! We may not just throw texts at each other with the words, 'But the Bible says . . .'

John Barton whose Lent book *Love unknown* helped many people two years ago has said about the Bible and moral decisions:

To read the Bible as literature, and for the most part great literature, is to recognise that we do not learn from it as we learn from a list of regulations. It is to be sensitive to the presence of many different genres within Scripture, only a few of which are described as 'teaching' at all. Whether or not we think we should 'obey' the directives in Leviticus or 1 Timothy, it is possible to see what it would mean to do so. But it is less clear in what sense one could 'obey' 1 Samuel or Lamentations or Acts! If these books are to work on our moral sense, it can only be in the way that other equally non-didactic literature does so; by informing our imagination and consciences; by making us sensitive to nuances and moral conduct; by presenting us with models and paradigms and analogies for our own action, and some understanding of the interplay of human desires and aspirations and conflicts.[5]

So we open our minds and hearts to the scriptures, the authority of the Church, the tradition, the art and literature which surrounds us, the experience and insights of our own lives and the lives of others, especially those less fortunate. And this is how, with God's help, we 'see' the way to go.

Norry McCurry, formerly rector of Stepney, is currently spiritual director at St James's, Piccadilly.

Notes

1. Nicholas Holton *Speaking Love's Name: Homosexuality* Some Catholic and Socialist Reflections (Jubilee Group, 1988).
2. *After Virtue* A study in Moral Theology (Duckworth, 1981).
3. In an address in St James's Piccadilly, October 1991.
4. *Paula Rego* Tales from the National Gallery by Germaine Greer and Colin Wiggins (National Gallery Publications, 1991).
5. *The Use of the Bible in Moral Debate* (Theology, May 1985).

'The King's good servant but God's first!'

David Alton

(This exclusive interview for Tracts for Our Times was given to Nicholas Kavanagh on 23 June 1992.)

David Alton, your public stance on such pro-life issues as abortion will be well known and appreciated by our readers. Would you like to say how your position on these issues of public morality is informed by your Christian faith?

WITH THE full force of British law we sanction every day the destruction of 600 unborn children, a total of nearly four million since the passage of the 1967 legislation. We sanction destructive experiments on the human embryo, we sanction the killing of the unborn baby even during birth if it has a minor form of handicap or disability. It shows how far secularism and utilitarianism have won the day. Even if as a Christian I were in a minority of one, that wouldn't allow me to remain silent on this issue.

When you look at what St Luke, a doctor, had to say in his account of the conversations he must have had with Jesus' mother, you can see where the inspiration for people like me comes from. Our Lord came into the world as an embryo, he was first greeted by a foetus in his mother's ageing cousin Elizabeth's womb. He chose not only to come as man but in the lowliest form of human life, the embryo. I think it's incumbent on us to have a deep and profound respect for all life; so, as a Christian, I think it's my duty to speak up on this issue, which I see as the supreme human rights question. Who is more voiceless, more powerless than the unborn child? I think it's very difficult for anyone who believes in a creator God, who believes we are fashioned in his likeness, made in his image, not to take this issue very seriously. When people tell me it is purely a matter of personal choice, I think a Christian has to dispute that. We can't be utilitarians. We can't say it's the lesser of two evils; for many of us it's the greater of two evils, and if a thing *is* evil, it should be challenged anyway.

But you don't have to be a Christian to be pro-life. What brings me great encouragement is that people from other faiths, including Islam and Buddhism, and some with no faith, are increasingly coming to see that, from the destruction of human life, stem many of the other degradations we see today in our society.

Are you impressed by the concept of a 'consistent ethic', a phrase used by Cardinal Bernadin of Chicago, meaning that Christians should not be selective in their pro-life attitudes? Should not the whole spectrum and context of human life be defended and dignified? What other issues, as well as abortion, do you see as a part of this consistent ethic?

Respect for life must be 'from the womb to the tomb'. The temptation is to be *anti* abortion rather than pro-life, to take a negative rather than a positive stance. The single-parent mother must be treated with dignity. We must not stigmatise, hurt or make life difficult for her, but support her in her decision to go ahead with the birth of the child. We must defend the poor and those who are oppressed in other situations: all this is consistent with pro-life attitudes.

We must be concerned about dignity in dying and the rights of the terminally ill. Now, euthanasia is a probability in this country. There is an all-party group in parliament keen to promote its legislation. We must be involved in this. In Holland, last year, three per cent of all deaths were accounted for by euthanasia.

Respect of life and social justice go hand in hand. The consistent ethic Cardinal Bernadin spoke of is a seamless garment.

You are a liberal democrat. What influenced your choice of party and how does this affect your pro-life views?

My mother was from the West of Ireland, which I'm sure explains a lot about me, but my father is a cockney by birth as indeed I am. He worked on the shop floor at Ford's, supported the Labour party and was involved in his trade union. I became politically interested as a youngster at school. There came the passage of the 1967 abortion act, the American involvement in the Vietnam War, the famine in Biafra, the Russian invasion of Czechoslovakia. These events all influenced my choice of party. I remember writing to the then leader of the Liberal party, Jo Grimmond, to ask whether the abortion issue was a matter of conscience or party policy, for David Steel, a liberal, had been the prime mover in the 1967 legislation.

I became a liberal, am now a Liberal Democrat, but I've never regarded my party as the communion of saints! I've always recognised its fallibility and that there will always be questions on which I disagree with them. Politicians and party members behave sometimes like football supporters on the terraces where their team can do no wrong. I'm in the party that, for me, offers the least worse option. Political parties are like human beings, earthen vessels. If you expect them to be perfect you'll be badly disappointed.

You are, of course, a member of parliament for a particular constituency, with a responsibility to represent the views of your constituents as well as the freedom to vote according to conscience. Does this cause conflict for you?

St Thomas More was always trying to square his political responsibilities with his conscience and looking for a let-out clause which would enable him to continue to hold a position of high political authority and to continue to serve the king.

But, ultimately, he couldn't do this. 'The king's good servant but God's first,' was what he said. If a person believes conscience matters and systematically destroys that conscience the person ends up destroying himself. The more politicians compromise, the more pragmatism takes the place of principle. The more people are interested in careers, in positions, in being things rather than doing things, the more they turn their backs on conscience. For me conscience is first, constituents second, the party third. That's the order in which we should operate. My constituents know there will be times when I shall disagree with them: I can't be all things to all men, running with the hare and hunting with the hounds. At a general election they can change me for someone else if they decide my judgement is at fault or goes against their beliefs. This is what journalists were forecasting would happen at the last election because of my pro-life stand. But here I am, talking to you, two months later, in the House of Commons! My beliefs didn't stop even more people voting for me than before. What was demonstrated was that my constituents believed it was better to have someone they disagreed with who knew his own mind rather than one of those drifters who, in the words of W. S. Gilbert, 'Always vote at their party's call. And never think for themselves at all!'

Some MPs have attacked the tactics of pro-life organisations who use mass mailing to lobby in their interest. They say this distorts public opinion and threatens to turn politics into a 'single issue' business. What is your comment on this?

The way in which the pro-life issue is relegated as being utterly irrelevant to the average member of parliament – they simply do not want to know – ought to be the issue which Christians take on.

The occasional mailing of MPs is not significant. MPs get far more mail about fox hunting and scientific experiments with animals than about experiments on their own species. If a seal were washed ashore bearing a placard saying, 'Save unborn children', then people might start to see the inconsistency of taking a stand on rainforest and animals (even though I support them) but not on their own species. I don't think it's the pro-lifers who need feel on the defensive: rather they ought to be on the *off*ensive, criticising those who refuse to allow this issue to be debated; it's the issue that 'dare not speak its name'. The European Convention on Human Rights states quite explicitly that the fundamental right is the right to life, a right which is treated in a very cavalier way today.

Could you comment on the words of the Archbishop of York, who is on record as having said that as a Christian he is opposed to abortion and considers it sinful, but that in a 'pluralist' society he does not think it right to impose this view on others by law?

I was very disappointed by the Archbishop of York's speech during the debate in the House of Lords on the Human Fertilisation and Embryology Bill. The speech was used by every atheist, every

117

humanist, every supporter of abortion in the House of Commons who trotted out his speech. What was so offensive was that there were many Anglicans who are passionately pro-life and who were very badly let down by him. It's not my concern to interfere with the affairs of the C of E, but I hope there'll be a really profound debate about the rights of the unborn.

The present Archbishop of Canterbury when he was at Bath and Wells was one of the very first people to write to me words of encouragement when I brought in my Private Member's Bill to reduce the legal limit beyond which abortions could occur to 18 week gestation. I was very happy with this and when I learnt of his appointment to Canterbury I could only think 'this is good news for the unborn child'.

Would you be an advocate for a 'Bill of Rights' which enshrined pro-life values? Are these so important that they should be subjects for referenda?

It would very much depend what was in the bill. I used to think I was an advocate of such a bill and once spoke in favour of it at an Oxford Union debate; but, by the end of the evening, I had come to be more impressed by the arguments of the other side. I would like to see, first, a 'Charter of Human Responsibilities'.

What I don't want is a bill which will enshrine the rights of some people at the expense of others: that would be pretty worthless.

The word 'choice' comes from the Greek word *haeresis* which is also the root of the word heresy. Maybe we should stop talking about our 'right' to choose. Do we have a 'right' to go on consuming as if tomorrow will never come, do we have a 'right' to destroy the environment without an eye to the consequences, a right to destroy another person's life? But we see daily the placards saying: 'It's my right to choose!' No one would want to argue that individuals shouldn't have control over their own fertility, but what about the consequences of their actions? This is where the word responsibility enters. Every Right should be balanced by Responsibility and Duty, so we should start by widening the debate and incorporating the European Convention on Human Rights into British Statute Law.

Before the public were faced, in a referendum, with an issue such as euthanasia, there would need to be a more balanced debate on the subject, throughout the country, than we've had so far. The media are hopelessly loaded with people who do not allow us, the opposition, to put forward its point of view. I've been appalled at the attitudes of people, particularly in the BBC, who rarely allow the pro-life point of view a proper airing and when they do they find someone who is not guaranteed to produce the most sympathetic response.

I'd be nervous of having a referendum until we could ensure a more balanced debate than we've seen so far, with all the arguments presented properly.

Your readers will have seen on TV almost every medical operation known to mankind on science programmes, but not what's involved in abortion. You never see pictures of a child at 18 weeks' gestation with every organ in place, pumping 50 pints of blood a day. This is a human being, able to feel pain and reacting to sound and light. What happens to this human being, without any anaesthetic, is that it is dismembered, piece by piece. The effect on the foetus, on the mother, on the medical staff is something which should be part and parcel of any mature debate on what it is that people have the 'right' to do. Until we can ensure we have a balanced debate on the subject, I'd be reluctant to have a referendum.

In many discussions on morality it is customary to instance a series of 'liberalising' enactments and trends together: contraception, abortion, embryo experiments, *in vitro* fertilisation, homosexuality, divorce, euthanasia. The Church has a clear position on all of these issues – a negative one. Would you wish to make some distinction between those which should be the object of legal prohibition and those which should not?

The issue for Christians living in a pluralist society is not what you can force people to do or not to do, but how do you protect the innocent. Why Christians should take a strong view on abortion is that there in the womb is a new person who is entitled to our protection and respect.

I would support any legislation protecting a child, once it is born, against abuse; but the worst form of child abuse is the destruction of life *in utero*.

What people do, as they mature in life, is a matter for themselves, the laws of the land and, as Christians, the laws of the Church.

These are clear: chastity and celibacy if single, chastity and fidelity within marriage. It's not appropriate for the State to legislate on these issues, but it is appropriate for the Christian Church to preach about them. None of us is a saint and we're all aware of failings in our own lives. I don't believe these are areas about which laws should be made. Because a bishop fails in his vow of celibacy does not negate the value of celibacy any more than adultery negates the value of marriage. While I'd be very against a return to laws which involve the criminalisation and prosecution of homosexuals for example, we must not confuse the obligation to demonstrate compassion with the Church's obligation to hold fast to an ideal.

Many people in the U.K. have taken comfort from the belief that the British constitution somehow guarantees the place of gospel values in our society: in the Crown, in the presence of bishops in the House of Lords. In your experience is this true?

That the British constitution and the C of E as the Established church preserve gospel values in our society is an illusion that people cling to and I'm not sure it's very healthy for the C of E or anybody else.

The members of our Christian churches still form a majority among believers of any faith. The C of E should take a rôle in civic life and speak up for gospel values. But I think the C of E would be listened to anyway, whether established or not. Indeed, being established might mean, for some, that what is said is listened to with disdain or at least less respect. The Church of Rome in this country is not established, although it is, of course, in other countries, and in the U.K. I think it gains because of it.

Cardinal Hume is listened to because he's worth listening to, not because he's been recognised by the State and I would say his authority would be reduced if he suddenly became recognised.

I have one caveat – if disestablishment were to be turned into an attack on the C of E by secular opinion, I would not wish to be associated with it. I hope the Church will sort this out itself first and not give the impression of responding to secular pressure.

How would you advise lay Christians (and the clergy for that matter!) to give political substance to their concern for society which they express in prayer? People say 'I'm not political.' Is this a real option for Christians?

We're all political to some extent because we're called to be involved in the world around us. Our own salvation is not all that matters: we want to be concerned about the issues that affect our brothers and sisters. We must start by looking at the person of Jesus. He obviously wasn't the Hon Member for Galilee West! Jesus is the archetype, the blueprint for the way we should run our lives. He regularly spent time in prayer and combined this with an active engagement in the community. St Augustine put it well when he said we must pray as if the entire outcome depends on god, and work as if the entire outcome depends on us. That's the call to us. Think of Wilberforce and his crusade against what he saw as the greatest evil of his time, slavery, that one human being could own another. There were huge vested interests in slavery, but he took them on and did so with spiritual armour, having been attracted by the Wesleyan revival, the house church movement of the day. He gathered his forces around him in Clapham and they prayed together and worked together. It took them 40 years to win, but win they did.

Jesus was born into a harsh world. He would have seen people crucified by the wayside, he was familiar with militant nationalism, he also became aware very quickly of the unpopularity of his message. So Christians should not be afraid when it comes to the crunch. They chose Barabbas then – the result of an early opinion poll! Like many opinion polls today it produced the wrong answer!

I passionately believe all prayer is answered and I must not get disheartened if it's not answered in the way I would prefer or expect. The answer may not come in my life time. So I need patience and repentance. When we recognise that we are responsible, collectively or individually, for injustices that have taken place, we've got to start to put them right. Prayer is the greatest weapon we've been given and we under-use it.

Would you like to say something about the Movement for Christian Democracy? How would you distinguish this Movement from a Christian Democrat Party on the continental model?

The Movement for Christian Democracy has six principles: a respect for life, social justice, active compassion, good stewardship, empowerment, and reconciliation.

These are woven together in the Westminster Declaration. It's inter-denominational and inter-party and there are regional groups. This is where its strength lies – in drawing people together. You can't have a respect of life without social justice! Up-and-coming campaigns include a report on the elderly and another on homelessness. The Movement has links with Christian Democracy in both western and eastern Europe, but has ruled itself out of becoming a political party as such. However, I do believe we all need to look seriously at the beliefs of Christian Democracy and ask whether they are needed in this country. They believe in:

Personalism, which is the idea that we are all individuals who should be allowed to and encouraged to do what we want, not that our future lies in corporation and the state, but the idea that the human personality 'made in the image of God' means that we are not just expendable raw material but entitled to dignity and self-respect. Personalism is there at the heart of the way we treat people.

Communitarianism, which is eventually a system which allows nations to work out their differences without recourse to war. I'd much rather we were arguing about ECUs and butter mountains rather than that young men were killing each other for the third time in a century.

Subsidiarity, the idea that decisions should be taken at the lowest possible or most appropriate level is the vision of a Europe of regions.

Solidarity, based on Catholic Social Teachings in *Rerum novarum* and *Quadragesimo anno*.

These are ideas which fit in with an authentic appreciation of the gospel. Thirty-five million people voted for these Christian Democracy ideals at the last European elections and their programme was opposed to embryo experimentation, opposed to abortion apart from where the person's life was at risk, and opposed to genetic engineering.

None of the British parties has a word to say about these questions. We have to understand what Christian Democrats have to offer. A lot of the Social Charter, much maligned in Britain, is their work. Profit-sharing schemes, becoming popular here, have been going for 20–30 years in countries like Germany.

Part of the Movement's purpose is to understand the Christian Democracy of the rest of Europe better.

Finally, you are on record as saying: 'We are the only country in Europe without a political movement founded on Christian ideals.' I think that many Christians would be mortified (perhaps rightly) to be told that their political allegiance was not already based on Christian ideals. Could you say something more about this?

Individual Christians are justifiably proud of the traditions and tap roots of whichever party they belong to: the Conservatives to Wilberforce, the Liberals to Gladstone, the Socialists to Keir Hardie. But it would be hard for anyone to disagree that, since the Second World War, each of the parties has drifted off into a different form of secularism. The Labour Party came to worship at the shrine of the State and abandoned much of its Christian heritage. As recently as 1991 the Labour pro-life group was actually banned, expelled from the party, deregistered. Now, if you cannot even allow a tiny group within your party to adopt a contrary view on the issue of abortion, then it says something about your intolerance and the extent to which you are removed from traditional Christian thinking. Abortion is not a matter of conscience to Labour Party members, it's now a matter of policy. The Liberal Party was traditionally a party of nonconformism and deeply rooted in the chapels of our land. But, since the Second World War, it's drifted more and more to the belief that we can solve all our problems by ourselves, through technocracy; for some members of the party there's been an attraction to New Age thinking and the more paganistic elements of the Green movement: building an altar unto ourselves and deifying man. There's a real temptation in liberalism to the belief that you don't need God, only yourself. The Conservatives went to a different extreme: a belief in materialism, 'do unto others before they do you' has become a parody of the gospel and Mrs Thatcher's assertion that there's no such thing as Society seems to sum it all up. The reinterpretation of the Parable of the Good Samaritan makes the moral of the story the fact that you have money in your pocket in the first place.

Christians who are members of any one of the parties need to look very closely at where they have gone and work for a return to their Christian roots. It'd certainly be very good for them and the country. Equally the parties should not be surprised if a Christian movement arises to challenge the secularism of the age. We're not setting ourselves up as a moral majority but we are saying: 'This is where our country's going and we don't like the direction.'

David Alton is Liberal Democrat Member of Parliament for Liverpool, Mossley Hill constituency.

Bibliography

Iain Mackenzie

THIS SHORT bibliography has two sections: recent titles on moral theology and ethics, and recommendations from our authors for further reading.

Recent Titles

Tom L. Beauchamp & James F. Childress *Principles of Biomedical Ethics* (OUP, 1989)

L. William Countryman *Dirt, Greed and Sex: Sexual Ethics in the New Testament and their Implications for Today* (SCM Press, 1989)

Ed. Gordon R. Dunstan & E. A. Shirebourne *Doctors' Decisions: Ethical Conflicts in Medical Practice* (OUP, 1989)

Raymond Gaita *Good and Evil: An Absolute Conception* (Macmillan, 1991)

Robin Gill *A Textbook of Christian Ethics* (T & T Clark, 1985)

Anthony E. Harvey *Strenuous Commands: the Ethic of Jesus* (SCM Press, 1990)

Michael Keeling *The Foundations of Christian Ethics* (T & T Clark, 1990)

George Newlands *Making Christian Decisions* (Mowbray, 1985)

Ronald H. Preston *The Future of Christian Ethics* (SCM Press, 1987)

Alan M. Suggate *William Temple and Christian Social Ethics Today* (T & T Clark, 1987)

Peter Vardy *Business Morality* (Marshall Pickering, 1989)

(The publishers thank the Librarian, Sion College Library, Victoria Embankment, London EC4Y 0DN for providing this list of titles.)

Further Reading
The moral teaching of Jesus in the contemporary world
(Pages 11-24)

JOHN MACQUARRIE places particular value on Anthony Harvey's *Strenuous Commands (op.cit.)*, a strenuous read, too, but a very rewarding one nonetheless (a Bible should be at hand in order to consult the texts). Earlier chapters emphasise the impracticability of the teaching of Jesus in a world of getting and spending. He also recommends two further books, both from SCM Press, *Basic Christian Ethics* by Paul Ramsey (1953) and *A New Dictionary of Christian Ethics* edited by J. A. Childress and Dr Macquarrie himself (1990), which will appeal to the more specialist student.

The paschal mystery and the question of meaning (Pages 45-53)

NICHOLAS KAVANAGH introduces his article with a reference to Piers Paul Read's latest novel *On the Third Day*. This is available from Mandarin (1991). Five other books recommended are: *Law, Love and Language* by Herbert McCabe (Sheed & Ward, 1979); *The Resurrection and Moral Order* by Oliver O'Donovan (IVP, 1986); *Being Human* by Edmund Hill (Chapman, 1984); *The Lord's Dealing: the Primacy of the Feminine in Christian Spirituality* by Robert Faricey (Paulist Press, 1988); and *The Mystery of Christ* by Thomas Keating (Element Books, 1991).

Pride and Prejudices (Pages 64-72)

SISTER AGATHA MARY recommends two books: Paul Tournier's *The Violence Inside* (SCM Press, 1975) and *The Last Battle* by C. S. Lewis (Armada, 1980). This is the only reference to Lewis in the whole symposium. Twenty years ago a collection of essays on ethics might have been expected to contain almost as many allusions to the man who is said to have 'made righteousness readable'.

Living with violence (Pages 73-82)

MARTIN ISRAEL suggests one classic of soul-writing from the past half-century: Dietrich Bonhoeffer's *Letters and Papers from Prison*, first published by Collins in 1953 but frequently reprinted in Fount Paperbacks. *Letters and Papers from Prison* is one of those comparatively few books which should be regularly re-read, because it means more, more deeply each successive time. Two of Dr Israel's own recently published books are also commended: *The Dark Face of Reality* (Fount, 1989) and *The Pain that Heals* (Arthur Jones, 1992).

The churches in eastern Europe (Pages 83-93)

HUGH WHYBREW offers an excellent up-to-the-minute read to follow his article on the problems currently facing eastern European churches, Misha Gleny's *The Rebirth of History: Eastern Europe in the Age of Democracy* (Penguin, 1992). Misha Glenny is often heard on the radio for the BBC World

Service. His book contains many provocative thoughts on the underground church that has existed in Czechoslovakia and the fears of Catholic clergy in Poland that the new democracy will abolish their political function. Glenny pursues the line that what is needed are Christian Democratic parties on the model of those in Germany and Italy.

Here I stand! (Pages 104-113)

NORRY McCURRY recommends books which support his conviction that Christians should be taking a stand on difficult issues. Most recent is Kevin Kelly's *New Directions in Moral Theology* (Geoffrey Chapman, 1992). *A Textbook of Christian Ethics* by Robin Gill (T & T Clark, 1985) has a very good introduction, with texts and extracts from the Christian tradition. Alasdair MacIntyre's *After Virtue: A Study in Moral Theology* (Duckworth, 1982) and *Christian Ethics and Contemporary Philosophy* edited by Ian Ramsey (SCM Press, 1973) both have much to offer, especialy Chapter 11 of the latter, 'Vision and Choice in Morality' by R.W Hepburn and Iris Murdoch. Then there are the Iris Murdoch novels connecting aesthetics and moral decisions, including *The Bell* (Triad/Granada, 1981) and *The Sea, The Sea* (Penguin, 1989)

'The King's good servant but God's first! '(Pages 114-124)

DAVID ALTON quoting Thomas More goes to the heart of the dilemma of conscience and public service. Robert Bolt in *A Man for All Seasons* (Heinemann, 1960) effectively dramatised the problem.

Iain Mackenzie is a retired teacher of English who reviewed books regularly for the Church Times *between 1967 and 1989.*

The following titles in the St Mary's Bourne Street series **Tracts for Our Times** are available:

Volume 2 *In Vitro Veritas - More Tracts for Our Times*
0-9508516-1-2

Volume 4 *Signs of Faith, Hope and Love - The Christian Sacraments Today*
0-9508516-3-9

Volume 5 *Building in Love - The Vocation of the Church*
0-9508516-4-7

Volume 1 *Tracts for Our Times* and **Volume 3** *'If Christ be not risen...'* are out of print.

All titles in print can be ordered through any good bookshop and are distributed to the trade through SCM Press, 26-30 Tottenham Road, London N1 4BZ *(071-249 7262)*